Amazing YOU

KAYODE ADEKOLA

Published in the United Kingdom by Rory Manuel Publishing

ISBN: 978-1-9168849-0-8

ACKNOWLEDGEMENTS

I want to use this opportunity to express my profound gratitude to those who assisted me in making this piece of work a reality. Special thanks go to Pastor Joseph Olimah and Mr Bukola Adeyemi for their assistance during the period of editing this book. I would also like to appreciate Pastor Fatai Kasali for his advice and encouragement any time I called on him. May the Almighty God bless you all in Jesus name Amen.

My special appreciation to my wife, Temitope Dorcas and my children, Promise, Glory and Emmanuel for their encouragement and support when putting this book together.

Lastly, I would like to return all the glory to the Almighty God for sharing His light and wisdom with me to be able write this book.

Glory be to God! Hallelujah!

CONTENTS

Chapter ONE

INTRODUCTION - AMAZING YOU

This book, **Amazing You**, is to let you know that you are an amazing creation of God, wonderfully crafted together to achieve a divine purpose. You are not an accidental creature, no matter your background or the situation of your parents before you were born. You have been brought to this cosmic earth to fulfil a divine agenda.

Psalm 139:14-18 (KJV) says 'I will praise thee; for I am fearfully *and* wonderfully made: marvellous *are* thy works; and *that* my soul knoweth right well. My substance was not hid from thee, when I was made in secret, *and* curiously wrought in the lowest parts of the earth. Thine eyes did see my substance, yet being unperfect; and in thy book all *my members* were written, *which* in continuance were fashioned, when *as yet there was* none of them. How precious also are thy thoughts unto me, O God! how great is the sum of them! *If* I should count them, they are more in number than the sand: when I awake, I am still with thee.

David appreciated the goodness of God for his creation. He said that God saw his form even when he was still being formed in his mother's womb; he concluded by saying that God's thoughts towards him were precious and that he could not put a number to the glorious thoughts God had for him. Child of God, God has wonderful and glorious thoughts concerning you. He wants you blessed, successful and achieve his divine plan for your life.

The scripture says in:

> **Jeremiah 29:11 (KJV) For I know the thoughts that I think toward you, saith the LORD, thoughts of peace, and not of evil, to give you an expected end.**

This promise of God is Amazing! Isn't it? This promise of God is for every child of God, not just a few. If you are born again, God has amazing thoughts concerning you.

When I look at the Oxford English Dictionary meaning of ***Amazing***, I see definitions such as:

Great surprise or wonder, astonishing, very impressive, excellent etc.

Child of God, you are created for wonders, to flourish and to make an indelible impression in this world. If only you will find God's purpose for your life, pursue it with all the vigour you have got within you, then you will be a wonder to your world in Jesus name, amen.

Despite this glorious plan of God for His children, people generally compare themselves with others, they compare themselves to their colleagues and friends who are prospering in their endeavours and they wish to be like them. Nothing wrong in wanting to prosper, after all, the scripture says in **3 John 2 (KJV)** Beloved, I wish above all things that thou mayest prosper and be in health, even as thy soul prospereth.

However, what happens in most cases, is that people want to be like other people forgetting that each person has been created for a different purpose.

Many would like to be like Mark Zukerberg, Facebook founder or Oprah Winfrey, one of the most influential women in the world. If you look at the two individuals I mentioned above, you will realise that the two of them are not recognised in the world for doing the same thing, neither is their net worth the same. Mark Zukerberg has a net worth of $99.6 billion according to Wikipedia while Oprah Winfrey's net worth is put at $2.5 billion. Mark is known as a social media entrepreneur while Oprah is known as a media executive and a talk show host. They are both well-known but pursue different dreams.

A world where everyone is a multi-millionaire or billionaire is a fantasy that is not rooted in reality. Let us take a look at another personality, though late, Mother Teresa received a Nobel Peace Prize in 1979 for her humanitarian works. I tried to check her net worth, but nothing was recorded of her in money terms because she lived all her life for charitable purposes. You would not consider her a failure just because she was not rich in money terms. She impacted others through her charitable deeds and fulfilled her God-given potentials.

The above notwithstanding, as a child of God, God's intention for you is that you are successful, blessed and achieve his divine purpose for your life. It is not God's plan that you fail, and you will not fail in Jesus' name, amen. However, please note that being successful and blessed should not be measured **only** in amount of dollars or pounds you have stored in the banks, but in the lives you touched, those that you put smiles on their faces and whether or not you released all that God has put within you. That should be the measure of success!

When you study the bible, you will know that despite the fact that both John the Baptist and Jesus Christ were called to ministry of preaching the gospel, they were however created to achieve different purpose. John the Baptist was a fore runner of Jesus Christ. He knew that he was not the Messiah and he did not attempt to be one.

When the Jewish leaders sent priests and temple assistants to him to ask if he was the Messiah, he retorted with a capital No……I am not the Messiah. In fact, they asked him if he was Elijah or the prophet they were expecting. His answer for the two questions was No. When they probed him further so that they could give a reply to the Jewish leaders that sent them, John the Baptist replied I am a voice shouting in the wilderness, Clear the way for the Lord's coming **(John 1:19 -23)**.

John's purpose was different from that of our Lord Jesus Christ. Christ knew that his purpose was to go to the cross and shed his blood for the remission of the sin of the world. Christ did not depart from God's purpose for his life. He committed his life to achieving this purpose even when it was difficult to do so.

The same can be said of other bible characters, they all had different purposes, and so do you. You need to discover this purpose and pursue it.

This book is to make you know that God's purpose for you is good and that he has put within you all that you need to achieve all that he created you to be. You are a phenomenon already, an amazing creation of God. You can excel, you can soar high and succeed, and achieve God's purpose for your life. This book will attempt to explain how you can realise your God-given potentials.

Please follow me on this journey as I unravel to you the steps you need to take to realise the Amazing You.

Chapter TWO

AMAZING YOU THROUGH AMAZING GRACE

The wicked are too proud to seek God, they seem to think that God is dead (**Psalms 10:4**). Many could not realize their true potentials because of barrage of problems that confront them, hence, they stop trying when faced with multitude of challenges, some even take their own lives as a result of issues of life. Do you know that everyone on the surface of the earth has got one problem or other? No one is immune from problems. However, when problems are overcome, then that is what give rise to testimonies!

The difference between the believer and the unbeliever is that one puts his trust in God and seeks him to resolve all problems of life. The unbeliever does not know God and therefore does not seek after God. When unbeliever has problem, he puts his trust in created things:

Romans 1:25 (ASV) for that they exchanged the truth of God for a lie and worshipped and served the creature rather than the Creator, who is blessed forever. Amen.

This book is titled the AMAZING YOU. To be amazing is to live an enviable life, a life that will give glory to God, in short you might want to call it a life that is filled with amazing testimonies. Testimonies are divine interventions in the life of a child of God.

The bible is full of amazing testimonies that God is alive and does amazing things for those that put their confidence in him. You too can have amazing testimonies that would make you awe struck and when you tell the story, many will find it difficult to believe, I pray that this will be your testimony as you have decided to read this book.

Many amazing testimonies are recorded in the scriptures to give us hope and encouragement as we wait patiently for the promises of God to be fulfilled in our lives (**Romans 15:4).** For instance, the children of Israel encountered the Red Sea as they attempted to flee from slavery in Egypt which they had been for over 400 years. We read that even the Sea had to flee, parted, and congealed so that his children could walk on the seabed, however, when the army of Pharaoh attempted to do the same, they were capsized by the sea. Is that not amazing! This book is about how you too as a child of God can experience this type of amazing testimonies in your personal life. God promised that he will always make a difference between his children and those that serve him not **(Malachi 3:18)**.

The scripture (Bible) is replete with different kinds of stories of the awesome intervention of God in people lives especially in the lives of his children. Many wrongly assume that as believers, we should be immune from problems and challenges of life, but not even Lazarus, the one whom Christ loved, was free from challenges as he was attacked by sickness:

> **John 11:3 (KJV)** Therefore his sisters sent unto him, saying, Lord, behold, he whom thou lovest is sick.

Hence, both believer and unbeliever alike face the problems and challenges of life:

> **1 Corinthians 10:13 (KJV)** There hath no temptation taken you but such as is common to man: but God *is* faithful, who will not suffer you to be tempted above that ye are able; but will with the temptation also make a way to escape, that ye may be able to bear *it.*

However, while the unbeliever does not seek after God, because he does not have a relationship with God, the story of the believer is different, the believer can receive divine help to solve all his problems. That divine help is what is referred to as **Amazing Grace.**

Hebrews 4:16 (KJV) Let us therefore come boldly unto the throne of grace, that we may obtain mercy, and find grace to help in time of need.

Grace in the Christian parlance means **unmerited favour, mercy, kindness, help etc.** when a man lacks grace, that means the person lacks favour, he receives no mercy, no kindness, or any help for that matter and that is a dangerous place to be. In John 5, a man was at the pool of Bethesda, sick and bedridden for 38 years, even though the pool had the potency to make him whole, but because there was no one to help him, he could not receive his healing. Therefore, for you to be the AMAZING YOU, that God intended when he created you, you need to connect to that grace of God, the scripture says Know that the Lord, He is God; it is He who made us, and not ourselves; We are His people and the sheep of His pasture (**Psalms 100:3**).

God is our manufacturer; no manufacturer makes any product without a specific purpose. Therefore, for us to fulfil our purpose, we must know God's purpose for our lives, it is only when we know his purpose that we can fulfil it.

The question then is, how do you know God's purpose for your life?

There are so many ways you can know God's plan or purpose for your life, some of the ways could be as follows:

1. DIVINE REVELATION

When you look at the Bible, God himself revealed His plan to some people. Joseph as a young boy had a glimpse of his future. He saw in a vision of the night the sun, the moon and the eleven stars bowed down to me. This dream happened on two occasions in different versions. God revealed this to him so as to instruct him concerning his future.

Job 33:15-17 (KJV) In a dream, in a vision of the night, when deep sleep falleth upon men, in slumberings upon the bed; Then he openeth the ears of men, and sealeth their instruction, that he may withdraw man *from his* purpose, and hide pride from man.

Moses also knew the plan of God concerning his life by divine revelation. In the case of Moses, it was by divine manifestation of a rare occurrence of a burning bush. Moses had been zealous about the people of Israel; in fact, he became a fugitive because he committed a crime of murder by killing an Egyptian. When Moses saw the bush burning and the bush not consumed, he said to himself, this is a rare occurrence, let me turn around and take a closer look. The moment he approached the burning bush, he heard the voice of God.

Exodus 3:4 (KJV) And when the LORD saw that he turned aside to see, God called unto him out of the midst of the bush, and said, Moses, Moses. And he said, here *am* I.

That day Moses received from God, his divine plan for his life.

Exodus 3:10 (KJV) Come now therefore, and I will send thee unto Pharaoh, that thou mayest bring forth my people the children of Israel out of Egypt.

2. SPIRITUAL PERCEPTION AND GODLY COUNSEL

In the case of Samuel, his mother had made vow to God that he was going to be dedicated to the service of God. Samuel's mother made the vow to God in her prayers; when she requested God to bless her with a son. Hannah, Samuel's mother, kept her word and fulfilled her vow by taking Samuel to Eli immediately when he was old enough to serve in the temple.

Samuel had been under the tutelage of Prophet Eli and Almighty God attempted to get Samuel's attention by calling him three times, however, Samuel erroneously thought that it was Eli that was calling him. Eli then perceived that it was the Lord that called the boy.

1 Samuel 3:8 (KJV) And the LORD called Samuel again the third time. And he arose and went to Eli, and said, here *am* I; for thou didst call me. And Eli perceived that the LORD had called the child.

Job 33:14 (KJV) For God speaketh once, yea twice, *yet man* perceiveth it not.

Samuel could have missed the call of God upon his life if not due to the maturity, counsel and experience of servant of God in the person of Eli. Therefore, if you are a child of God, know for sure that God is more than willing to reveal his will and plan for your life. You may not have perceived it yet; when you have such doubt in your heart, it is time to approach a more spiritual person or leader that you respect or your pastor for guidance as such a time like this.

That experience of Samuel confirmed to him and all the people of Israel that he has been set aside a prophet for the land.

1 Samuel 3:19-20 (KJV) And Samuel grew, and the LORD was with him, and did let none of his words fall to the ground. And all Israel from Dan even to Beer-sheba knew that Samuel *was* established *to be* a prophet of the LORD.

God also reveals his plan for our lives by our daily experiences. These experiences could be a pointer to the direction God wants us to pursue, it could be that you are suddenly drawn to a particular interest or you are losing interest in endeavours that used to excite you. At that time, if you open your spiritual antenna to the Lord and also approach him in prayers, you may perceive in your spirit man, that God is trying to get your attention to pursue a particular line of action, just like he did to Moses.

Jeremiah 23:18 (KJV) For who hath stood in the counsel of the LORD, and hath perceived and heard his word? who hath marked his word, and heard *it*?

3. INNER WITNESS OF THE HOLY SPIRIT

As children of God, we know we are born again because the Holy Spirit in us confirm or witness to our spirit that we are children of God.

Romans 8:16 (KJV) The Spirit itself beareth witness with our spirit, that we are the children of God:

> When you are tempted to do some bad things, you hear in your spirit man, you can no longer do some of those bad stuff you used to engage in. You have that inner witness because of the Holy Spirit that now dwells within you. If you are not a child of God, you will never have such an experience.

In the same vein, when you are interested in knowing God's plan for your life, you have the Holy Spirit communicating with your heart and spirit man in the form of an inner witness:

> **John 10:27 (KJV)** My sheep hear my voice, and I know them, and they follow me.

God continually speaks to his sheep, if you are one, he does that by communicating to our hearts:

> **Isaiah 30:21 (KJV)** And thine ears shall hear a word behind thee, saying, this *is* the way, walk ye in it, when ye turn to the right hand, and when ye turn to the left.

Revelation 3:20 (KJV) Behold, I stand at the door, and knock: if any man hear my voice, and open the door, I will come in to him, and will sup with him, and he with me.

When you continually hear a voice in your heart/mind, take this direction or call this person etc and you know you have not prompted it by yourself, it could be the Lord speaking to you in your inner self of a particular action that you need to take.

4. THROUGH THE WORD OF GOD

God also speaks through his infallible word if you are a regular reader of the word of God. You may get to some verses of the scriptures that appear to address your circumstance at the time. Some of the verses may allay your fear, for instance, there was a time in my life that I lost my job and I was concerned about what the future holds. I was concerned that the future was bleak, no hope in the horizon. I began to do some odd jobs and after a while I decided to separate myself in prayers because I needed God to speak directly to my situation. After I finished my fasting and prayers, I decided to pick up the bible to read, lo and behold I began to read Isaiah 49 and when I got to verse 20, it was like God himself coming down to speak directly to my situation, after reading the passage below, I started weeping, this is because it was so direct, spot on and addressed my most important worry at the time.

Isaiah 49:20-21 (KJV) The children which thou shalt have, after thou hast lost the other, shall say again in thine ears, the place *is* too strait for me: give place to me that I may dwell. Then shalt thou say in thine heart, who hath begotten me these, seeing I have lost my children, and am desolate, a captive, and removing to and fro? and who hath brought up these? Behold, I was left alone; these, where *had* they *been*?

The passage above, when I interpreted it at the time, it was like God saying to me, my son do not worry, I am in control, the things you will have after the loss of your job will be so great, that you will begin to ask yourself, who has brought this up?

Brethren, God is real, and he loves us, and he is very much interested in speaking to his children. I can tell you affirmatively, that it happened exactly as it was spoken to me. I later got a job in the middle east; my salary was tax free and I did that job for a couple of years thereafter. Glory to God! Hallelujah!

5. GOD SPEAKS THROUGH CIRCUMSTANCES

The situations of our lives are a pointer to the direction God intends to lead his people. Look at Paul and Silas embarking on their missionary journey in Asia. On two separate occasions they attempted to preach the gospel in those two places, but they were prevented by the Holy Spirit. It was not the devil that hindered them from preaching.

Acts 16:6-7 (KJV) Now when they had gone throughout Phrygia and the region of Galatia, and were forbidden of the Holy Ghost to preach the word in Asia, after they were come to Mysia, they assayed to go into Bithynia: but the Spirit suffered them not.

God could intervene in a particular situation and caused a door to close. You may do everything within your power and the door could still remain closed.

Revelation 3:7 (KJV) And to the angel of the church in Philadelphia write; These things saith he that is holy, he that is true, he that hath the key of David, he that openeth, and no man shutteth; and shutteth, and no man openeth;

When that happens, God is letting you know that is not the direction I intend for you. However, when God is leading you to take a direction in life, he alone knows how to open that door for you. Let us look once again to Paul and Silas, after repeated closed doors. They eventually experienced an open door that no one could shut.

Acts 16:9-10 (KJV) And a vision appeared to Paul in the night; There stood a man of Macedonia, and prayed him, saying, come over into Macedonia, and help us. And after he had seen the vision, immediately we endeavoured to go into Macedonia, assuredly gathering that the Lord had called us for to preach the gospel unto them.

When it was God's plan for Paul and Silas to take the gospel to Macedonia, he opened a door that no power of hell could close. I believe God that everything that God has in stock for you will come to you in Jesus name, amen.

When we were pursuing the purchase of our church building, we saw a mighty intervention of God. We saw God opened door for us in an incredible way. Few months after we completed the purchase of the building, I had a chat with some members of the church that sold the building to our church. These members told me that for many years they attempted to convert the building to flats and they also prayed that God should make it possible. Each time they presented their proposal to the Council, they met a brick wall. After our church became successful in the tender process of acquiring the church building, they then realised that it was not God's plan to convert that old church building to residential apartments. It was God's plan for the building to remain as church building. That church building that I am referring to is now owned by the Redeemed Christian Church of God, Victory at Reading (It was built and dedicated in 1899). This building was purchased because God himself worked out the testimony.

6. GOD SPEAKS THROUGH GIFTS

1 Peter 4:10 (KJV) As every man hath received the gift, *even so* minister the same one to another, as good stewards of the manifold grace of God.

God has a purpose for everyone especially his children, it will not be making sense that you are not gifted in what the Almighty God desired that you accomplish on the earth. Therefore, your gifts, talents and natural endowment could be signs of what your assignments are on the surface of earth.

Exodus 35:30-33 (KJV) And Moses said unto the children of Israel, See, the LORD hath called by name Bezaleel the son of Uri, the son of Hur, of the tribe of Judah; And he hath filled him with the spirit of God, in wisdom, in understanding, and in knowledge, and in all manner of workmanship; And to devise curious works, to work in gold, and in silver, and in brass, and in the cutting of stones, to set *them*, and in carving of wood, to make any manner of cunning work.

The gifts that God gave to him are reflection of his calling. Many people who are gospel singers, preachers, basketball players and footballers discovered their calling and assignments in life based on the heavenly gifts that God showered on them from birth.

Jeremiah 1:5 (KJV) Before I formed thee in the belly, I knew thee; and before thou camest forth out of the womb I sanctified thee, *and* I ordained thee a prophet unto the nations.

When you look closely to the gifts of God in your life, things that other people will struggle to do, however, when it comes to you, that is done with ease or effortlessly. This could give you a divine direction of what your future holds.

I must at this point let you know that there is no one that is without a gift. You may have to look within you closely to discover it. Gifts differ from another; everyone has got a gift that is different from that of another. You also have your gift from the Lord. It may be in public speaking, cooking, gardening etc All you need to do to shine is to discover and develop that gift.

Paul had to encourage Timothy not to neglect the gift that was in him:

> **1 Timothy 4:14 (KJV)** Neglect not the gift that is in thee, which was given thee by prophecy, with the laying on of the hands of the presbytery.

God wants to help us, he wants us to enjoy his amazing grace, he has designed us from the foundation of the world to shine for him. The word of God says we are his masterpiece, you know when Architects design building, they had a beautiful building in mind when designing buildings for their clients. God of heaven says, child of God, I have designed you to be a masterpiece. God is saying that what I had in mind is glorious, excellent, wonderful and that is what is going to be your testimony in Jesus name, amen.

Ephesians 2:10 (KJV) For we are his workmanship, created in Christ Jesus unto good works, which God hath before ordained that we should walk in them.

God is very much interested in revealing his plan to you; he wants to speak to us on a regular basis. However, before this can be possible, he wants you to know him on a relational basis. Therefore, if you have not surrendered your life to Jesus Christ, you can do that right now by confessing your sins and taking this prayer with me.

Father I repent of my sins, I confess them to you, please forgive and pardon me of them all. I believe that Jesus, the Son of God, died for my sins and he rose again for my justification. I believe I am now a child of God. Please give me the power to live for you in Jesus name, amen.

If you have taken the prayer above, you are now a child of God and you are on your way to realizing the AMAZING YOU.

Chapter THREE

CREATE ATMOSPHERE FOR YOU TO SEE AMAZING YOU

Amazing you will not manifest except you create an atmosphere for it to come to manifestation. What atmosphere do you need for this to happen?

1. AVOID JEALOUSY AND UNREASONABLE COMPARISON

Every man is different. Adam was formed by God from the earth, while Eve was formed from Adam's ribs. No two persons are exactly the same. We have all been born different, even twins though could be identical in looks, they are still different in may be temperament, heights, body weights etc. Let us look at Esau and Jacob in the bible:

> **Genesis 25:24-26 (KJV)** And when her days to be delivered were fulfilled, behold, *there were* twins in her womb. ***And the first came out red, all over like an hairy garment; and they called his name Esau.*** And after that came his brother out, and his hand took hold on Esau's heel; and his name was called Jacob: and Isaac *was* threescore years old when she bare them.

Esau was a hairy man, but Jacob was not. They were born same day by the same mother and yet they are different in looks and they also serve different purposes, because they had different purposes, they were blessed with skills different from another:

> **Genesis 25:27 (KJV)** And the boys grew: and Esau was a cunning hunter, a man of the field; and Jacob *was* a plain man, dwelling in tents.

Esau was a skilled hunter while Jacob was a man of quiet temperament, preferring to stay at home. Child of God, for you to become an amazing you God intends you to be, you must love yourself the way the Almighty God created you. You must be happy in your skin, you must love everything about yourself, your intellect, height, look, body weight etc. Stop comparing yourself with another. Everything you need to be whom God has destined you to be is within you. You have got all you need to prosper, flourish and breakthrough in life.

2 Corinthians 10:12 (KJV) For we dare not make ourselves of the number, or compare ourselves with some that commend themselves: but they measuring themselves by themselves, and comparing themselves among themselves, are not wise.

Many cannot be become amazing personalities that God intends them to be because they are looking at others with their gifts and talents, then when they look at themselves, they fail to see that which God has given them to succeed. They conclude in themselves, oh I have no gift, I have no talents, I am deprived, I do not see myself making it. If you continue to believe that lie, it will be very difficult for you to blossom.

Look at John the Baptist, he never compared himself with our Lord Jesus Christ. They both were preaching and baptising. John the Baptist never compared himself with Christ. He was comfortable with whom God had called him to be. He knew God's purpose concerning his life and he pursued it to a logical conclusion. When the Jewish leaders came to him to ask whom he was, he replied thus:

> **John 1:20 (KJV)** And he confessed, and denied not; but confessed, I am not the Christ.

He told the Jewish leaders, he was not Christ, and he was not also trying to make people believe he was Christ. When he was pressed further to find more about him, he replied:

> **John 1:23 (KJV)** He said, I *am* the voice of one crying in the wilderness, Make straight the way of the Lord, as said the prophet Esaias.

John the Baptist knew his purpose was to usher in our Lord and Saviour Jesus Christ into his ministry and John the Baptist did exactly that. He never tried to claim to be Jesus. He never tried to conduct his ministry like that of Jesus. He was comfortable in his own skin. In fact, at a later stage, when people were trying to compare him with Jesus, people said to him more people were going to Jesus for baptism and you were the one that baptised him.

John 3:27-28 (KJV) John answered and said, A man can receive nothing, except it be given him from heaven. Ye yourselves bear me witness, that I said, I am not the Christ, but that I am sent before him.

John the Baptist went further:

> **John 3:29-30 (KJV)** He that hath the bride is the bridegroom: but the friend of the bridegroom, which standeth and heareth him, rejoiceth greatly because of the bridegroom's voice: ***this my joy therefore is fulfilled. He must increase, but I must decrease.***

John the Baptist could not have made the statement above if he were not happy with whom God has destined him to be. Brethren, the point I am trying to make is that we are not equally gifted, we do not have the same destiny, be happy with whom you have been created to be and pursue your destiny with joy.

Let me give you another example in the scripture, Jonathan, the first son of Saul, he had been in the army before David; if you look at it from hereditary point of view, being the first son of king Saul, he should be entitled to the throne after his father's death. However, Jonathan could see the hand of God upon David, that David had been destined to the throne of Israel. Jonathan did not allow that to bother him. Jonathan never attempted to stop David to get to the throne. He was comfortable with God's plan for his life. At a point, Jonathan was a great encourager to David in all of his trouble with king Saul. He assured David, that God, will keep his words and David was going to become the king of Israel:

> **1 Samuel 23:17 (KJV)** And he said unto him, Fear not: for the hand of Saul my father shall not find thee; and thou shalt be king over Israel, and I shall be next unto thee; and that also Saul my father knoweth.

Jonathan never struggled in competition with David for the throne. He kept his own lane and he was happy with whom God created him to be. Child of God, God has given all you need to fulfil your destiny. Stop looking at what your friends have, stop desiring their gifts and talents. Look within yourself and you will discover that you have got your own gifts and talents to succeed and you shall succeed in Jesus name.

Look at Cain in the scriptures, he allowed hate and Jealousy to take root in his life and that was why he committed murder. Cain committed murder just because the Almighty God accepted Abel's gift and God rejected his own. If Cain did not allow hate and jealousy to take root in his heart; he would have concluded, this year it was Abel's time. Goodluck to Abel, I will improve on my gift next year, peradventure God will also accept my gift. When you refused to accept whom God has created you to be, it may lead you to do that which is unthinkable; you may refuse to use the gift that God has given you and lose out on your destiny.

The story of the parable of the talents come in handy here, the man that received one talent, kept it, and refused to use it. Even that one talent which he had was taken from him and was given to the one that had ten talents.

Matthew 25:28 (KJV) Take therefore the talent from him, and give *it* unto him which hath ten talents.

Yes, it is true that we have received different talents, some have 5 talents, some 2 talents, as long as you use yours, you will see an increase in Jesus name, amen.

King Saul though was the king of Israel, was not comfortable with whom God had made him. When the women of Israel began to sing, Saul had killed his thousand and David had killed ten thousand; Saul allowed that to create hate and jealousy in his heart. He abandoned that which God had given and began to pursue another, whom he perceived was destined to the throne after him. Please appreciate what God has given you, thank him for your gifts and talents and pursue your God-given destiny. You will succeed in Jesus name, amen.

2. PLANT YOURSELF IN A GOOD SOIL

The scripture in Psalms 92 says the godly shall be planted in the court of our God, while in Psalms 1, the bible says the godly shall be like a tree that is planted along the riverbank:

> **Psalm 92:13 (KJV)** Those that be planted in the house of the LORD shall flourish in the courts of our God.

Psalm 1:3 (KJV) And he shall be like a tree planted by the rivers of water, that bringeth forth his fruit in his season; his leaf also shall not wither; and whatsoever he doeth shall prosper.

You must recognize that humans are formed from a seed (man seed mixing with woman seed is what produces man) hence for you to succeed as a child of God, you must plant yourself deliberately in an atmosphere that will accentuates your gifts and talents. Stop hanging around those that refuse to see God's gifts and hands upon your life. All they see about you are negative stuff; daily it is all about criticism of what you are not doing right. If you continue to hang around such people, you will lose confidence in your own abilities. There is no one that is perfect, when a child is attempting to walk, many times he will fall but he does not stop trying. When he falls, he rises up again and continues until he reaches a point when he perfects the art of walking.

Proverbs 24:16 (KJV) For a just *man* falleth seven times, and riseth up again: but the wicked shall fall into mischief.

Does it mean that I am saying you should not listen to criticisms? No, that is not what I am saying. If criticisms are positive, wanting to get the better part of you, then that is alright, you can bring those type of criticisms on board. However, there are some criticisms that are borne out of jealousy, just like Saul against David. Those are the ones that you need to discard, do not entertain them, because if you do, they will stop you from getting to the place of your greatness.

Every great person that has achieved God's purpose for their lives have all been heavily criticised. Joseph was criticised by his brothers in Genesis 37:8 "So you think you will be our king, do you? Do you actually think you will reign over us? And they hated him all the more because of his dreams and the way he talked about them". Moses was not any different, when Moses tried to separate two Hebrew brothers who were involved in a conflict; Moses said to the man who had started the fight, why did you strike your fellow? The man replied, "who appointed you to be our prince and judge?" The statement was unkind to a man attempting to broker peace between two brothers that were fighting. Therefore, no matter who you are, know fully well that people will attempt to criticise you, say all sorts of evil things against you. If you are a man of destiny, you will just ignore them. That was what Saul did when he became the king, and some people refused to bring him gifts, they said among themselves, how can this one rule over us?

1 Samuel 10:27 (KJV) But the children of Belial said, How shall this man save us? And they despised him, and brought him no presents. But he held his peace.

Whatever you are trying to achieve; you must be criticised. The kingdom of darkness will also send his agents against you to stop you. You must, however, not succumb to their antics and threats. You must not give up; you must not yield any ground to the wicked one. You must stand your ground, though things appear as if you are yet to get to your destination, be persistent, don't give in to discouragement and you will see your desire coming together in Jesus name, amen.

When you deliberately surround yourself with people who wish you well, who encourage you, then you are bound to produce fruits in thirty and one hundred folds in Jesus name, amen.

Matthew 13:8 (KJV) But other fell into good ground, and brought forth fruit, some an hundredfold, some sixtyfold, some thirtyfold.

3. AVOID PRIDE

God is always in business of lifting people especially his beloved, which you are one if you have given your life to Jesus:

> **Psalm 3:3 (KJV)** But thou, O LORD, *art* a shield for me; my glory, and the lifter up of mine head.

God took David from just a shepherd boy straight into the palace:

> **Psalm 78:70-71 (KJV)** He chose David also his servant, and took him from the sheepfolds: From following the ewes great with young he brought him to feed Jacob his people, and Israel his inheritance.

The same applied to Joseph, he was taken from the prison and made a premier in Egypt. That is the wonderful works of God. You also can be lifted. The bible says God is no respecter of person. When your own time comes, the Almighty God will also lift your head to a place of honour in Jesus name, amen.

After God has lifted your head, you have to be careful to avoid pride, this is because pride destroys:

> **Proverbs 16:18 (KJV)** Pride *goeth* before destruction, and an haughty spirit before a fall.

Even though God lifts, God also brings down:

> **Psalm 75:6-7 (KJV)** For promotion *cometh* neither from the east, nor from the west, nor from the south. But God *is* the judge: he putteth down one, and setteth up another.

Look at Haman in the scriptures, he was lifted above all the other chiefs in Susan, but he allowed pride into his life, and that was what brought him down. Whatever height that you are lifted, brethren, please avoid pride, it is a plague that destroys:

> **James 4:6 (KJV)** But he giveth more grace. Wherefore he saith, God resisteth the proud, but giveth grace unto the humble.

When you are proud, you are reminding God what Satan did in heaven before he was brought down:

> **Isaiah 14:12-15 (KJV)** How art thou fallen from heaven, O Lucifer, son of the morning! *how* art thou cut down to the ground, which didst weaken the nations! For thou hast said in thine heart, I will ascend into heaven, I will exalt my throne above the stars of God: I will sit also upon the mount of the congregation, in the sides of the north: I will ascend above the heights of the clouds; I will be like the most High. Yet thou shalt be brought down to hell, to the sides of the pit.

Brethren, pride is like a cancer that destroys quietly, you may not realise it until it is very too late. Look at Nebuchadnezzar, through the help of Jehovah, he was able to build his kingdom to a place of honour, he refused to acknowledge the help of God, he began to exalt himself:

> **Daniel 4:30 (KJV)** The king spake, and said, Is not this great Babylon, that I have built for the house of the kingdom by the might of my power, and for the honour of my majesty?

Nebuchadnezzar was brought down until he realised that God rules in the affairs of men:

> **Daniel 4:32 (KJV)** And they shall drive thee from men, and thy dwelling *shall be* with the beasts of the field: they shall make thee to eat grass as oxen, and seven times shall pass over thee, until thou know that the most High ruleth in the kingdom of men, and giveth it to whomsoever he will.

Child of God, please avoid pride so that the blessings of God upon your life can endure forever.

4. AVOID SINFUL HABITS

Pride could be subtle, not being evident. However, sinful habits are not hidden. Many have been destroyed by sinful lifestyles. God is holy and wants us, his children, to also be holy:

> **1 Peter 1:15-16 (KJV)** But as he which hath called you is holy, so be ye holy in all manner of conversation; Because it is written, Be ye holy; for I am holy.

Samson was brought down and destroyed because of lack of self - control and engaging in sinful lifestyle. Samson was severally warned of his lifestyle, but he refused to take to the warning until it was too late for him:

> **Judges 16:30-31 (KJV)** And Samson said, Let me die with the Philistines. And he bowed himself with *all his* might; and the house fell upon the lords, and upon all the people that *were* therein. So, the dead which he slew at his death were more than *they* which he slew in his life. Then his brethren and all the house of his father came down, and took him, and brought *him* up, and buried him between Zorah and Eshtaol in the burying place of Manoah his father. And he judged Israel twenty years.

Samson had a great destiny, but he died prematurely, what a tragedy! When you engage in sinful habits, you are inadvertently inviting curses and wrath of God upon your life.

Sin destroys anyone who engages in it, the scripture says that God is holy and cannot behold sin:

> **Colossians 3:5-6 (KJV)** Mortify therefore your members which are upon the earth; fornication, uncleanness, inordinate affection, evil concupiscence, and covetousness, which is idolatry: For which things' sake the wrath of God cometh on the children of disobedience

The word mortify means to put to death. Therefore, any of your members that wants to put you in a position that will attract the wrath of God, put it to death.

Matthew 5:29 (KJV) And if thy right eye offend thee, pluck it out, and cast *it* from thee: for it is profitable for thee that one of thy members should perish, and not *that* thy whole body should be cast into hell.

5. ALWAYS BE POSITIVE

In life, there will always be challenges. Things will come against us that may challenge our faith. We should however be positive irrespective of negative darts coming from our world or even from the kingdom of darkness wanting to stop us from our goal. We should be confident of our God to work out things ultimately in our favour:

> **John 16:33 (KJV)** These things I have spoken unto you, that in me ye might have peace. In the world ye shall have tribulation: but be of good cheer; I have overcome the world.

David was close to his becoming king when Ziglag was attacked by the Amalekites. Things were so bad, that the people spoke of stoning him. Everyone around David was depressed and sad. David instead encouraged himself in the Lord:

> **1 Samuel 30:6 (KJV)** And David was greatly distressed; for the people spake of stoning him, because the soul of all the people was grieved, every man for his sons and for his daughters: but David encouraged himself in the LORD his God.

When things are not what you expect, when you are working so hard and you are seeing little results, please at that point in time, be positive, encourage yourself in the Lord your God, this Is because God has promised never to leave us or forsake us:

> **Hebrews 13:5 (KJV)** *Let your* conversation *be* without covetousness; *and be* content with such things as ye have: for he hath said, I will never leave thee, nor forsake thee.

Even when people come against you to thwart your efforts, never take revenge, never give up, always be positive. This is exactly what David did. King Saul was after David's life and all in an attempt to stop him from getting to the throne. David had opportunity twice to kill King Saul, but he refused to take revenge:

> **1 Samuel 24:4-6 (KJV)** And the men of David said unto him, Behold the day of which the LORD said unto thee, Behold, I will deliver thine enemy into thine hand, that thou mayest do to him as it shall seem good unto thee. Then David arose, and cut off the skirt of Saul's robe privily. And it came to pass afterward, that David's heart smote him, because he had cut off Saul's skirt. And he said unto his men, The LORD forbid that I should do this thing unto my master, the LORD'S anointed, to stretch forth mine hand against him, seeing he *is* the anointed of the LORD.

> **1 Samuel 26:12 (KJV)** So David took the spear and the cruse of water from Saul's bolster; and they gat them away, and no man saw *it*, nor knew *it*, neither awaked: for they *were* all asleep; because a deep sleep from the LORD was fallen upon them.

David, on these two occasions, was in close proximity with Saul and if he had wanted to kill him, he would have killed him. David waited patiently in all his battle against Saul until his prayers were answered. When David time came, the people themselves came to him to ask him to become king. Nothing then could stop him:

> **2 Samuel 5:2-3 (KJV)** Also in time past, when Saul was king over us, thou wast he that leddest out and broughtest

in Israel: and the LORD said to thee, Thou shalt feed my people Israel, and thou shalt be a captain over Israel. So, all the elders of Israel came to the king to Hebron; and king David made a league with them in Hebron before the LORD: and they anointed David king over Israel.

6. BE PRAYERFUL

The scripture says God works in mysterious ways:

Isaiah 45:15(NLT) Truly, O God of Israel, our Saviour, you work in mysterious ways

The ways of God are past finding out. One of the strategies of reaching your goal is to commit your ways to the Lord:

Proverbs 3:5-6 (KJV) Trust in the LORD with all thine heart; and lean not unto thine own understanding. In all thy ways acknowledge him, and he shall direct thy paths.

Prayer does wonders, if you can leverage on the power of prayers, you will find doors opening up miraculously:

Jeremiah 33:3 (KJV) Call unto me, and I will answer thee, and shew thee great and mighty things, which thou knowest not.

Many have used this great spiritual resource when in trouble, to achieve God's plan for their lives. You also can deploy this great resource to solve all your problems and realise your goals.

Peter was in prison and the church began to pray. Suddenly God sent an angel to go to the prison and get Peter out of the prison, that is what prayer can do:

Acts 12:5 (KJV) Peter therefore was kept in prison: but prayer was made without ceasing of the church unto God for him.

To those who know the power of prayers, they have always used it to their advantage:

> **Daniel 2:18-19 (KJV)** That they would desire mercies of the God of heaven concerning this secret; that Daniel and his fellows should not perish with the rest of the wise *men* of Babylon. Then was the secret revealed unto Daniel in a night vision. Then Daniel blessed the God of heaven.

Daniel and his other brothers were in Babylon, a strange land, they knew God. When they found themselves in trouble, they deployed the power of prayers which rescued them from the power of the enemy. Prayer works, so use it to your own advantage as well.

7. AIM HIGH

One of the reasons people do not attain to their full potentials is because of their limited thoughts; they are complacent with where they are. They are not striving to go higher. The Israelites on their way to the promised land found themselves spending about 38 years around Kadesh Barnea, they were probably not thinking any longer to go ahead and possess the land the Lord their God had for them. They were encircling around mount Seir and were almost getting satisfied remaining at mount Seir:

> **Deuteronomy 1:6-8 (KJV)** The LORD our God spake unto us in Horeb, saying, Ye have dwelt long enough in this mount: Turn you, and take your journey, and go to the mount of the Amorites, and unto all *the places* nigh thereunto, in the plain, in the hills, and in the vale, and in the south, and by the sea side, to the land of the Canaanites, and unto Lebanon, unto the great river, the river Euphrates. Behold, I have set the land before you: go

> in and possess the land which the LORD sware unto your fathers, Abraham, Isaac, and Jacob, to give unto them and to their seed after them.

In essence, God was saying to the children of Israel that there were still mountains to be surmounted, this is not your final destination, do not settle down here. The Lord your God would still give the mountains of the Canaanites, the Amorites, and the other nations that he promised you. He specifically told them they must be prepared stretch themselves by not settling at mount Seir, they must take their journey to the place God promised them.

No matter where you are now, God still have better plans for your future. However, you must be prepared to stretch yourself:

> **Isaiah 54:2-3 (KJV)** Enlarge the place of thy tent, and let them stretch forth the curtains of thine habitations: spare not, lengthen thy cords, and strengthen thy stakes; For thou shalt break forth on the right hand and on the left; and thy seed shall inherit the Gentiles, and make the desolate cities to be inhabited.

When you stretch yourself, you are giving yourself the opportunities to enlarge or move to the next level. People lose out on opportunities because, when they are supposed to make preparation for the next level of their lives, they did nothing and therefore when the opportunity comes, they are not prepared for it. No matter your area of calling, look for opportunities to be better at what you do, learn new skills, innovate, educate yourself either through formal or informal education. Just do not sit down, thinking that you have arrived at your destination. There are still opportunities to move up and you will move up in Jesus name, Amen.

8. BE KNOWLEDGABLE

Daniel 1:20 (KJV) And in all matters of wisdom *and* understanding, that the king inquired of them, he found them ten times better than all the magicians *and* astrologers that *were* in all his realm.

Daniel and his friends were found to be ten times better than their contemporaries even though they were in a foreign land and therefore they could serve in the king's palace. If you want to excel in life, you must also excel in knowledge. Joseph was able to get to the position of Prime Minister in Egypt because he provided solution to the king's problem. In fact, not just the king's problem but he provided solution to the problem of the entire nation. He could not have done that without knowledge. In your chosen field, search for knowledge. In times we live in it is easier to have knowledge in any area of your choice by using the power of the internet. Now, you have various search engines such as Google, Bing, Fire Fox etc and you can also learn from various social media platforms such as Facebook, Twitter, YouTube etc. All you need is to create interest and you can have the entire world of knowledge in your palms.

Also note that knowledge does not just mean knowing something, knowledge becomes knowledge when it can solve practical problems. Look at Jesus when he had to feed over 5000 men in the wilderness with just five loaves of bread and two fishes.

John 6:5-6 (KJV) When Jesus then lifted up *his* eyes, and saw a great company come unto him, he saith unto Philip, Whence shall we buy bread, that these may eat? And this he said to prove him: for he himself knew what he would do.

When the disciples saw the crowd, they did not know what to do at that point in time, but not Jesus. He knew what to do.

John 6:9 (KJV) There is a lad here, which hath five barley loaves, and two small fishes: but what are they among so many?

Jesus had a problem-solving skill, everyone that came to Jesus for help, did not go home disappointed, whatever the nature of their problem, whether lack, oppression from Satan, sicknesses and diseases, he met all their needs. That is the purpose of knowledge, to solve problems:

> **Mathew 15:30 (NLT)** A vast crowd brought to him people who were lame, blind, crippled, those who could not speak, and many others. They laid the before Jesus, and he healed them all. The crowd was amazed! Those who had not been able to speak were talking, the crippled were made well, the lame were walking, and the blind could see again! And they praised the God of Israel.

You too should learn from Jesus, seek to use your knowledge in a practical way. Once, you solve problems, the journey to realising amazing you is just very close.

9. HANDLE SETBACKS WISELY

When you look at people who have achieved great success in life, you might wrongly assume that they never at any time faced tough times. Truth be told, the way to the top is laden with a lot of difficulties and setbacks. Many who have achieved great success overcame great obstacles. They saw obstacles as steppingstones to reach the top. If you also want to reach the top, you have to look beyond your present circumstances, you have to see obstacles as temporal. Please have at the back of your mind that obstacles are to be overcome. Let us look at David and his journey to become great. David at age of 17 was ordained as the king of Israel, however, he did not attain that feat of becoming king until the age of 30. David, between the intervening years had great difficulties and great setbacks. At one time, he had no permanent home, he could only afford to live in the cave or on the street. At another time, his home was set on fire by the Amalekites. All these happened to a man that was destined for the throne. He handled setbacks wisely. David later said:

> ***2 Samuel 22:36 (NLT)*** You have given me your shield of victory; your help has made me great.

Therefore, if you see yourself having great difficulties, know that everyone that desires to get to the top goes through the same, but do not lose your confidence in the Lord, he will turn things around for you in Jesus name, amen

10. PREPARE FOR DISLOYALTY

Loyalty according to English dictionary means commitment, steadfast, reliable, faithful etc. Loyalty is difficult to find among people, Proverbs 20:6 Many will say they are loyal friend, but who can find one who is truly reliable. In your quest to become amazing, know for sure that not everyone will be committed to your vision. Not everyone will wish that you realise your dreams, in fact, some will even attempt to scuttle it. That was the case of Joseph and David, men tried to stop them from getting to their destinies. Those men that tried to stop them failed. I believe also that whoever tries to stop your progress or your dream, will also fail as long as you stay with the Almighty God.

Romans 8:31 (KJV) What shall we then say to these things? If God *be* for us, who *can be* against us?

Look at David's own father, Samuel asked him to invite all his sons to the sacrifice, and Jesse left David out. What can be more disloyal than that? Jesse could not stop God's plan for David. Joseph's brother also could not stop the plan of God for Joseph. I believe God that no matter how terrible disloyalty you face, by the grace of God, you will overcome in Jesus name if you stick with God. I have never seen God abandon those whose hearts are loyal to him.

2 Chronicles 16:9 (KJV) For the eyes of the LORD run to and fro throughout the whole earth, to shew himself strong in the behalf of *them* whose heart *is* perfect toward him. Herein thou hast done foolishly: therefore from henceforth thou shalt have wars.

Chapter
FOUR

AMAZING YOU THROUGH HARD WORK

In chapter one, I spoke about two individuals, Mark Zuckerberg, and Oprah Winfrey, even though, these two accomplished individuals may not be born again but they have distinguished themselves in their vocations. God expects his children to even be more successful. He wants you prosperous even as your soul prospers.

One of the ingredients that you will need, as a child of God, to realise your amazing you is hard work. Even though God wants you blessed and prosperous, if you refuse to work hard to make that dream come true, it will just be an illusion that does not come to manifestation.

Proverbs 12:14 (KJV) A man shall be satisfied with good by the fruit of *his* mouth: and the recompense of a man's hands shall be rendered unto him.

The scripture is always true. The passage above says that a man will be recompensed by the work of his hands. Whatever you do is what you get back, if you bring zero to God, even if God multiply your zero, it will still be zero at end of the day. The scripture says that he that sows sparingly, will also reap sparingly. Even though we always use this scripture when it comes to giving and receiving from God, it also applies to the work of your hand. God will bless whatever you bring to him.

Let us examine the story of the widow of a man of God (2 Kings 4: 1-8), the man of God Elisha advised her to borrow vessels from her neighbour, he specifically mentioned to her not a few. The oil she got from that miracle was dependent not just on oil but also on the number of borrowed vessels she borrowed.

2 Kings 4:6 (KJV) And it came to pass, when the vessels were full, that she said unto her son, Bring me yet a vessel. And he said unto her, *There is* not a vessel more. And the oil stayed.

If this widow had borrowed more vessels, she would have received more as well. Jacob also was a blessed and prosperous man, but he also laboured for Laban, his master, even though they were related, Jacob laboured for Laban.

Genesis 31:42 (KJV) Except the God of my father, the God of Abraham, and the fear of Isaac, had been with me, surely thou hadst sent me away now empty. God hath seen mine affliction and the labour of my hands, and rebuked *thee* yesternight.

Brethren there is no substitute for labour, you cannot shine for Jehovah without hard work:

Proverbs 12:24 (KJV) The hand of the diligent shall bear rule: but the slothful shall be under tribute.

Proverbs 12:24 (NLT) Work hard and become a leader; be lazy and become a slave.

Having established the need for hard work, how then does God expects us to work?

1. WORK WITH PLANNING

2 Chronicles 27:6 (KJV) So Jotham became mighty, because he prepared his ways before the LORD his God.

When work is not properly planned, then there is no blueprint to follow, the result could be haphazard, that is why it is very necessary before you set out for each day, week, month or even year, have a plan in place on what you want out of that day, week, month or even year. It becomes a guide that you can use to measure your success. In the construction industry, performance is measured by a programme of work, project managers and planners know when a project is ahead or behind schedule, whatever is the case there are control measures within the projects to adjust whenever it is required.

2. WORK WITH DETERMINATION

Nehemiah 6:9 (KJV) For they all made us afraid, saying, Their hands shall be weakened from the work, that it be not done. Now therefore, *O God*, strengthen my hands.

Nehemiah approached the rebuilding of the wall of Jerusalem with great determination to succeed. Many people put obstacles on his way to ensure that he did not succeed, but because he was determined, every obstacle thrown at him was a stepping to achieving his dream.

Genesis 11:6 (KJV) And the LORD said, Behold, the people *is* one, and they have all one language; and this they begin to do: and now nothing will be restrained from them, which they have imagined to do.

If you look at the above passage in New American Standard Translation, the word "imagined to do" is replaced with "purpose to do". That means nothing can stop a determined mind. God always open up a way where it appears there is no way to a determined mind. If God could open up a way for the Israelites at the Red Sea, then what will be too difficult for him? Absolutely nothing!

3. WORK WITH ENTHUSIASM

Ephesians 6:7(NLT) Work with enthusiasm, as though you were working for the Lord rather than people.

If you want to see the hands of God on your life or your business, do your work from the heart and with great enthusiasm. Even though, you may be working for an individual or organization, in actual sense you are working for God. He wants you to do your work with great happiness. If you are unhappy in the job you are doing currently, pray to God for divine intervention and God will make your dream to come to pass in Jesus name, amen.

It may mean that you may have to retrain into another sector that you are interested in. When we relocated to Ireland in 2005, my wife was working as a health care assistant; she never felt fulfilled in that role; she made up her mind to change direction. She applied to do adult nursing for another 4 years and she had to drive for 4 hours every day for the next four years. She never complained because that was her dream. Today, she is happy that she made that decision. You too can look at your life, prayerfully consider your options and take a decision as you are led by the Holy Spirit. You must approach your work daily with enthusiasm

4. WORK MUST BE DONE CORRECTLY

1 Chronicles 28:20 (NLT) Then David continued "Be strong and courageous and do the work. Don't be afraid or discouraged for the Lord God, my God is with you. He will not fail you or forsake you. He will see to it that all the work related to the Temple of the lord is finished correctly.

Whatever God does he does it correctly. When God created the universe and looked at the work of his hands, he said they were "very good". This is a cue for us as his children that half-baked work, substandard work should not be traced to us.

When king Nebuchadnezzar looked at Daniel and his friends and other people who were meant to serve in the king's palace, they were found to be ten times better:

Daniel 1:20 (KJV) And in all matters of wisdom *and* understanding, that the king inquired of them, he found them ten times better than all the magicians *and* astrologers that *were* in all his realm.

5. FINISH THE WORK

John 17:4 (KJV) I have glorified thee on the earth: I have finished the work which thou gavest me to do.

God never left any work unfinished, so also Jesus never abandoned any assignment given to him. No matter how difficult, Jesus completed and finished all that was required of him from his father; even to the point of going to the cross:

John 19:30 (KJV) When Jesus therefore had received the vinegar, he said, It is finished: and he bowed his head, and gave up the ghost.

One of the ways of knowing a lazy man is that he leaves things uncompleted, he procrastinates, I will do it tomorrow, I will do it next tomorrow and so on. Therefore, a lazy man cannot achieve the dream that God has for him no matter how lofty.

Proverbs 12:27 (KJV) The slothful *man* roasteth not that which he took in hunting: but the substance of a diligent man *is* precious.

6. SHARPEN YOUR SKILLS

The world keeps changing, it has been said that skills of yesteryears may not be good for the present not to even talk of that of the future. Prior to year 2000, little is known about social media. The same applies to computers, there was a time that people trained on typewriters, but now with the advent of computers, such skills are no longer required:

One of the features of the end time is that knowledge will increase:

Daniel 12:4 (KJV) But thou, O Daniel, shut up the words, and seal the book, *even* to the time of the end: many shall run to and fro, and knowledge shall be increased.

The times we are in require that you must look for opportunities, reskill or retrain, otherwise, you may realise that you are obsolete, and you are no longer relevant to the present age:

> **Ecclesiastes 10:10 (KJV)** If the iron be blunt, and he do not whet the edge, then must he put to more strength: but wisdom *is* profitable to direct.

I heard about a story of a fisher man who for many years had been using a particular frying pan to fry the fishes she gets from the river, one of her customers one day sat in front of her while she fries the fishes. She then noticed that anytime she caught large fishes, she put them back into the river. When she gets a small fish, she fries them. This customer being curious asked the fisher man, I noticed that when you caught a big fish, you threw it back in the river and you only fry the small fishes. The fisher man replied I throw back the big fishes in the river because I have a small frying pan that can only fry small fishes. The man was dazed, he said to him you may as well just change your frying pan and fry big fishes and that would mean more profit for you. The fisher man said I never thought of it. That is the position that some of us as children of God find ourselves. Do not be stuck doing the same thing, over and over again without finding out, how that vocation, business can be done better. Always think on how to innovate!

In conclusion for this chapter, work will always bring profit, do not run from hard work:

> **Proverbs 14:23 (KJV)** In all labour there is profit: but the talk of the lips *tendeth* only to penury.

God wants to reward your work, so child of God, put your heart to your work and you will be generously rewarded:

> **2 Chronicles 15:7 (KJV)** Be ye strong therefore, and let not your hands be weak: for your work shall be rewarded.

Chapter
FIVE

AMAZING YOU THROUGH DIVINE INTERVENTION

Amazing You may not manifest just because you have surrendered your life to the Lord Jesus Christ. However, your believing in our Lord Jesus Christ is a condition precedent or a precursor to realising God's plan and purpose for your life.

There are so many people who are born again and yet they are still languishing under the yoke of the wicked one. Some are still under sicknesses and diseases; some are still being tormented with fears, anxieties, and depression. If these conditions are in your life, you cannot be said to be enjoying the AMAZING YOU that God has designed for you. You need divine intervention for you to realise the AMAZING YOU.

Let us look at the man that had been bed ridden for 38 years in the bible. This man's name was not given; however, we know that this man had been in that state for so long. There was no intervention from man nor from God, that was why he stayed in that condition for far too long.

This man could not be said to be enjoying his life, abundant life that God promised was far from him. His prosperity was tampered with by the power of darkness, he was far away from being victorious over the wicked one. However, things changed for him the moment he received divine intervention. It was an amazing testimony! He went from being sick and depressed to being totally healed and free from the yoke of the enemy. All this happened to him same day because the Son of God intervened in his situation. He experienced a total turnaround.

Whatever is your situation right now, whether it is sickness, poverty and lack, no significant achievement in life etc, whatever it is; you need to approach God for a divine intervention.

Matthew 11:28 (KJV) Come unto me, all *ye* that labour and are heavy laden, and I will give you rest.

Once you approach the throne of grace, you will find help to solve all your problems in Jesus name, amen. The moment God intervenes, you are on your way to becoming the Amazing you. May this be your portion in Jesus name, amen.

Now Let us Look at why God changed the story of this bedridden man for good?

1. HE DESIRED A CHANGE

The first thing that a man who needs a change have to do to experience a miracle is to desire it. Without a strong desire for a change then it is difficult to experience a turnaround.

John 5:1-5 (ASV) After these things there was a feast of the Jews; and Jesus went up to Jerusalem. Now there is in Jerusalem by the sheep *gate* a pool, which is called in Hebrew Bethesda, having five porches. In these lay a multitude of them that were sick, blind, halt, withered, *waiting for the moving of the water for an angel of the Lord went down at certain seasons into the pool, and troubled the water: whosoever then first after the troubling of the* *waters stepped in was made whole, with whatsoever disease he was holden.* And a certain man was there, who had been thirty and eight years in his infirmity.

Jesus knew the man had been in that condition for a long time, if there was no desire for a change of situation the man would have given up and asked to be taken home. But the man was persistent, hoping that one day, his time would come, and he would experience a change, so he had a strong desire! He did not give up; he kept his hope alive.

Job 14:14 (KJV) .... all the days of my appointed time will I wait, till my change come.

Child of God, you too should never give up on God. Pray to God for a turnaround. Do not listen to the lie of that devil that God has forgotten you. You may see others having their own breakthroughs and thoughts could be coming to your hearts, that it will never happen. Please do not believe that thought, in fact, in most cases, God reserves his best to those who can wait for him. Look at the story of Hannah, she waited for the promised of God regarding childbearing. Hannah waited on God for a child and she gave birth to one of the greatest prophets in Israel. Child of God, you also should wait until your turnaround comes.

2. REALISED YOUR HELPLESSNESS

This bedridden man realised that he was helpless in his condition, that without an assistance, he would not be able to change his condition. He did not know who Jesus was and he probably recounting his ordeal of several failed attempts at his getting into the water, when the angel troubled the water.

John 5:6-7 (ASV) When Jesus saw him lying, and knew that he had been now a long time *in that case*, he saith unto him, Wouldest thou be made whole? The sick man answered him, Sir,

I have no man, when the water is troubled, to put me into the pool: but while I am coming, another steppeth down before me.

The man kept on dialoguing with the Lord, because he was very desirous of a change of situation.

Luke 18:1-8 (KJV) And he spake a parable unto them *to this end,* that men ought always to pray, and not to faint; Saying, There was in a city a judge, which feared not God, neither regarded man: And there was a widow in that city; and she came unto him, saying, Avenge me of mine adversary. And he would not for a while: but afterward he said within himself, Though I fear not God, nor regard man; Yet because this widow troubleth me, I will avenge her, lest by her continual coming she weary me. And the Lord said, Hear what the unjust judge saith. And shall not God avenge his own elect, which cry day and night unto him, though he bear long with them? I tell you that he will avenge them speedily. Nevertheless when the Son of man cometh, shall he find faith on the earth?

The widow kept troubling the Judge saying to him that "look; I am helpless, I cannot avenge this situation for myself, please help me" Therefore, for you to witness a change, you need to realise your helplessness and go to him that can help you.

Psalm 121:1-2 (KJV) A Song of degrees. I will lift up mine eyes unto the hills, from whence cometh my help. My help *cometh* from the LORD, which made heaven and earth.

Once you set your eyes on the Lord, then you are setting yourself up for amazing testimony and that will be your portion in Jesus name, amen.

3. BELIEVE THE WORD OF THE LORD

Jesus said to the man stand up, pick up your mat, and walk – that is a divine instruction from the Lord to this man. Remember this man is bedridden, if he refused to believe the word of the Lord and kept on saying I cannot, he would not have been a beneficiary of this miracle. However, he acted on the word of the Lord, he obeyed the divine instruction even though this is illogical to what he was experiencing. Until we act on the word of God and believe that it will work for us, we may not experience the miracle we desire.

Miracles and testimonies are birthed on the altar of believe. The scripture says if thou can believe, thou will see the glory of God (**John 11:40**). The bible is laden with good and precious promises that address every challenge of life and we just have to believe them as written word sent to us to deliver us from all problems of life. For instance, should you need healing, there is a scripture that says "I am the Lord that heals thee", you have got to believe this word, that Jesus purchased your healing on the cross, that when he died on the cross, he said it is finished to all works of the devil. You have got to believe it and have confidence in his word, just like you believe the word of your doctor that says you are now healed you can return home. You believe the doctor because the doctor is an expert in his field and Jesus also said all power in heaven and on earth has been given unto me and Jesus said I took your infirmities and bore your sicknesses and by my stripes you are healed. You have got to believe this and act on it and then you will see the manifestation.

When Jesus was approached by two blind men regarding their sight, Jesus asked them:

Matthew 9:28-29 (ASV) And when he was come into the house, the blind men came to him: and Jesus saith unto them, Believe ye that I am able to do this? They say unto him, Yea, Lord. Then touched he their eyes, saying, According to your faith be it done unto you.

Believe is what gives birth to miracles, no one can receive a miracle of any kind from God without faith. Let me show you a few examples here:

- ***The woman with the issue of blood:***
  Luke 8:48 (NLT) Daughter, he said to her, your faith has made you well. Go in peace.
- ***Gentile woman whose daughter was demon possessed:***
  Mathew 15:28 (NLT) Dear woman, Jesus said to her, your faith is great. Your request is granted. And her daughter was instantly healed.

In all the cases, they all witnessed amazing testimonies, because they believed the words of the Lord. Your testimony is hinged on your faith. The enemy will fight your faith and do everything possible to attack your faith in order to devour your testimony. You must not give in to the antics of the devil!

1 Peter 5:8-9 (KJV) Be sober, be vigilant; because your adversary the devil, as a roaring lion, walketh about, seeking whom he may devour: Whom resist steadfast in the faith, knowing that the same afflictions are accomplished in your brethren that are in the world.

4. REFUSED TO BE THROWN BACK TO HIS FORMER LIFE

After the man received his miracle, it is surprising to note that some people were still unhappy with this man receiving his testimony. Unfortunately, these were religious leaders they said to the man who was cured, you cannot work on the Sabbath! The law does not allow you to carry that sleeping mat! Unbelievable, this was said to a man who had been bedridden for 38 years.

You also must note that the powers of darkness are not happy that finally you have been let off the hook. When the children of Israel were freed from slavery in Egypt, Pharaoh did not just give up, they pursued after them.

Exodus 14:9-10 (KJV) But the Egyptians pursued after them, all the horses *and* chariots of Pharaoh, and his horsemen, and his army, and overtook them encamping by the sea, beside Pi-hahiroth, before Baal-zephon. And when Pharaoh drew nigh, the children of Israel lifted up their eyes, and, behold, the Egyptians marched after them; and they were sore afraid: and the children of Israel cried out unto the LORD.

Also, you also have to stand up against those powers:

1 Peter 5:9 (NLT) Stand firm against him, and be strong in your faith. This man who was once bedridden stood up against those religious leaders by declaring what Jesus told him.

John5:11(NLT) But he replied, The man who healed me told me, Pick up your mat and walk.

5. RETAIN YOUR VICTORY

Another thing that you need to do is to retain your healing. The power of darkness is not happy that you have received your amazing testimony. Therefore, you must do all within your powers to retain your testimony.

Now, let us look at how this man retained his healing:

John 5:14 But afterward Jesus found him in the Temple and told him, Now you are well, ***so stop sinning or something even worse may happen to you.***

There are many who have received their miracles and eventually lost it because they refuse to take heed to the advice above that Jesus gave to this man who used to be bedridden.

Luke 11:24-26 (KJV) When the unclean spirit is gone out of a man, he walketh through dry places, seeking rest; and finding none, he saith, I will return unto my house whence I came out.

And when he cometh, he findeth *it* swept and garnished. Then goeth he, and taketh *to him* seven other spirits more wicked than himself; and they enter in, and dwell there: and the last *state* of that man is worse than the first.

Therefore, to keep your miracle and testimony, please keep from all appearance of the enemy, and your testimony shall be permanent in Jesus name, amen.

Chapter **SIX**

DIVINE INSTRUCTIONS TO RECEIVE AMAZING TESTIMONIES

The plan of God is that all His children should prosper and have amazing testimonies.

3 John 2 (KJV) Beloved, I wish above all things that thou mayest prosper and be in health, even as thy soul prospereth.

Mark 16:20 (KJV) And they went forth, and preached everywhere, the Lord working with *them*, and confirming the word with signs following. Amen.

Therefore, if you are a child of God, you are designed to succeed! If you look at the scriptures very well, you will understand that those that succeeded in their assignments were people who received divine instructions on what they needed to do to succeed.

For instance, God told Joshua after the death of Moses, you are the one who will lead these people to possess all the land I swore to their ancestors I would give them (Joshua 1:6); Joshua was told what he needed to do to experience the success that God intended for him:

> **Joshua 1:7-8 (NLT)** Be strong and very courageous. Be careful to obey all the instructions Moses gave you. Do not deviate from them, turning either to the right or to the left. Then you will be successful in everything you do. Study this book of instruction continually. Meditate on it day and night so you will be sure to obey everything written in it. Only then you will prosper and succeed in all you do.

God wanted Joshua to succeed in his new assignment. God wants all his children to succeed in all their endeavours. Whatever is your profession or calling, please note that God wants you to proper.

Psalm 1:1-3 (KJV) Blessed *is* the man that walketh not in the counsel of the ungodly, nor standeth in the way of sinners, nor sitteth in the seat of the scornful. But his delight *is* in the law of the LORD; and in his law doth he meditate day and night. And he shall be like a tree planted by the rivers of water, that bringeth forth his fruit in his season; his leaf also shall not wither; and whatsoever he doeth shall prosper.

If Joshua had failed in this new assignment it would not have been God's fault as he had told him expressly all that he needed to do to succeed in his new assignment. That is also true for us as his children, just like a father would want his children to succeed, so also God wants us to succeed in all our endeavours, this is because success is what gives him glory not failure, and you will not fail in Jesus name, amen.

> **Isaiah 42:8 (ASV)** I am Jehovah, that is my name; and my glory will I not give to another, neither my praise unto graven images.

HOW DID JOSHUA KNOW WHAT TO DO?

1. HE LEARNED UNDER MOSES

Joshua was a man that received instruction from Moses, **Joshua 1:13 (KJV)** Remember the word which Moses the servant of the LORD commanded you, saying, The LORD your God hath given you rest, and hath given you this land.

Joshua on many occasions received instructions from Moses. He was a man under authority just like the centurion said to Jesus: "I am a man under authority" so also Joshua took instruction from Moses, he was mentored by Moses, he received instruction by what he saw Moses do and how Moses related with God. Wherever, Moses went, Joshua was his able assistant, no wonder when there was a need for change of leadership, God had no one else to take over leadership from Moses but Joshua, the son of Nun.

Joshua 1:1-3 (KJV) Now after the death of Moses the servant of the LORD it came to pass, that the LORD spake unto Joshua the son of Nun, Moses' minister, saying, Moses my servant is dead; now therefore arise, go over this Jordan, thou, and all this people, unto the land which I do give to them, *even* to the children of Israel. Every place that the sole of your foot shall tread upon, that have I given unto you, as I said unto Moses.

Joshua followed rigorously every instruction of his leader, Moses. A man that cannot take instruction from his superior, will definitely find it difficult to take instruction from God. If you cannot take instruction from another that you can see, it will be difficult to take instruction from God that you cannot see.

Mathew 8:9A (NLT) I know this because I am under the authority of my superior officers……

This Centurion understood the power of authority. He subjected himself to those above him; hence, he himself was able to give orders to those under him, which they in turn obeyed. He said to Jesus, you do not need to come to my house, I know you as a man of great authority, you just speak the word, and my servant shall be healed. Jesus commended this man, as a man with great faith.

Child of God, you also can learn from those ahead of you. No matter your field of endeavours, learn from those who have succeeded in that field. Learn their positive attributes, you can also learn from their mistakes. That is why people have mentors, to avoid mistakes that others have made. As you do this, you will succeed in Jesus name, amen.

Joshua learned from Moses' error of sending 12 spies to the promise land, though these twelve were leaders, they were not people of faith. Through their utterances, they denied a vast majority of the people to get to the promise land.

Numbers 13:32-33 (KJV) And they brought up an evil report of the land which they had searched unto the children of Israel, saying, The land, through which we have gone to search it, *is* a land that eateth up the inhabitants thereof; and all the people that we saw in it *are* men of a great stature. And there we saw the giants, the sons of Anak, *which come* of the giants: and we were in our own sight as grasshoppers, and so we were in their sight.

When Joshua was to send spies to Jericho, he chose just two, that is wisdom! Though these two men were probably not leaders, they were filled with faith. Even though they were resisted, when they brought the report back to Joshua, look at what they said:

> **Joshua 2:24 (KJV)** And they said unto Joshua, Truly the LORD hath delivered into our hands all the land; for even all the inhabitants of the country do faint because of us.

2. HE RECEIVED INSTRUCTIONS FROM THE LORD:

Joshua, having learnt leadership from Moses; he also knew that for him to succeed in the assignment God gave him, he must receive instructions from the Lord. Joshua was there when Moses received the tablets of commandments from the Lord on Mount Sinai. He was also among the spies that Moses sent to search out Canaan. Joshua saw at a distance, how God spoke to Moses from mouth to mouth like a friend speaks to his friend.

Numbers 12:8 (KJV) With him will I speak mouth to mouth, even apparently, and not in dark speeches; and the similitude of the LORD shall he behold: wherefore then were ye not afraid to speak against my servant Moses?

Joshua had been an ardent follower of God even when Moses was the leader of the people of Israel. He knew how to trust God even when others who went with him to spy the land of Canaan failed to fully depend on God to give them the land, only Joshua and Caleb fully trusted the Lord to give them the land.

Joshua 14:7 (KJV) Forty years old *was* I when Moses the servant of the LORD sent me from Kadesh-barnea to spy out the land; and I brought him word again as *it was* in mine heart.

At this point in his life, Joshua must have been God's favourites to lead the people of the Lord to the promise land. When God, eventually, told Moses he will not lead the people to the promise land, God told Moses:

Numbers 27:18 (KJV) And the LORD said unto Moses, Take thee Joshua the son of Nun, a man in whom *is* the spirit, and lay thine hand upon him;

Numbers 27:20-21 (KJV) And thou shalt put *some* of thine honour upon him, that all the congregation of the children of Israel may be obedient. And he shall stand before Eleazar the priest, who shall ask *counsel* for him after the judgment of Urim before the LORD: at his word shall they go out, and at his word they shall come in, *both* he, and all the children of Israel with him, even all the congregation.

To receive instructions from the Lord for your life, you need to do the following:

a. Wait for His Instruction:

God has promised to guide and instruct the meek, the reason God does this is that God does not want any of His children to be confused and not know what to do in any situation.

Psalm 25:9 (KJV) The meek will he guide in judgment: and the meek will he teach his way.

Psalm 32:8-9 (KJV) I will instruct thee and teach thee in the way which thou shalt go: I will guide thee with mine eye. Be ye not as the horse, *or* as the mule, *which* have no understanding: whose mouth must be held in with bit and bridle, lest they come near unto thee.

The period of waiting could be challenging as man could be in a hurry to take decision because of the pressure he is going through. At difficult time, I will advise that you do not take decisions in a haste as the scripture says he that believeth will not make haste. Impatience always lead to regret, so be careful.

Habakkuk 2:1 I will stand upon my watch, and set me upon the tower, and will watch to see what he will say unto me

b. Listen to His Instructions:

While you are waiting, you must listen in order to understand the instruction clearly, you may have to get your pen and paper out and write as he communicates with your spirit man.

Job 22:22 (NLT) Listen to his instructions and store them in your heart

Job 22:28 (NLT) Then you will succeed in whatever you choose to do, and light will shine on the road ahead of you.

Proverbs 16:20(NLT) Those who listen to instruction will prosper and those who trust the Lord shall be joyful

The purpose of listening is to know what to do, therefore once you are clear of the instruction of the Lord, the next thing is to act on what the Lord had told you.

c. Act on the Instruction:

It is the instruction that you act on that you can reap the benefits. If the Lord reveals anything to you, and you refuse to act on it, then you will regret not taking the action as instructed

Joshua 1:8 (KJV) This book of the law shall not depart out of thy mouth; but thou shalt meditate therein day and night, ***that thou mayest observe to do according to all that is written therein:*** for then thou shalt make thy way prosperous, and then thou shalt have good success.

God told Joshua that the purpose of this instruction that I am giving you is so that can do all, not some, that I am instructing you to do, then it is after your obedience is full that you can expect to see amazing testimonies.

John 2:5 (KJV) His mother saith unto the servants, Whatsoever he saith unto you, do *it.*

When wine got finished at the wedding in Cana in Galilee, even though the solution proposed by Jesus did not make any sense in that situation, but the servants who were in charge of serving wine at that party still went and obeyed the instruction of Jesus. Had they refused to obey; they would not have witnessed such an amazing testimony.

As a result of the servants' obedience, the Master of Ceremony not knowing that a miracle had just taken place said that everyone would set forth the good wine first and later that which is worse, but you have kept the good wine until later. An amazing testimony took place due to acting on instruction as given by the master **John 2:9-10 (KJV).**

The word of God as revealed in the bible is the mind of God. God wants you to know his mind on all areas of life and that is why he revealed them through the instrumentality of the scriptures. There are precious promises in the word of God already revealed unto us, God wants you to believe and act on these words, only then we can experience amazing testimonies.

2 Peter 1:4 (KJV) Whereby are given unto us exceeding great and precious promises: that by these ye might be partakers of the divine nature, having escaped the corruption that is in the world through lust.

DIVINE CONFIDENCE TO RECEIVING AMAZING TESTIMONIES

Confidence is required in all spheres of life. To become the amazing you that God plans for your life, a believer must demonstrate super confidence in God's ability to do exceedingly above and beyond all he can think or imagine. Without confidence in God, except by the mercies of God, it will be difficult for a child of God to see extraordinary hands of God in his life.

WHAT THEN DOES CONFIDENCE MEAN TO A BELIEVER?

1. TOTAL TRUST IN GOD

2 Corinthians 3:4-5 And we have such trust through Christ toward God. Not that we are sufficient of ourselves to think of anything as being from ourselves, but our sufficiency is from God.

The above scripture says that we put our trust in God through Christ Jesus. That we do not place our trust in ourselves, even though we may be well talented, equipped with different skills and gifts but all these can fail in times of great difficulties and challenges. The only one that is tested and true, that cannot fail is God.

Psalms 33:4(NLT) For the word of the Lord holds true, and we can trust everything he does.

God is ever faithful, trustworthy, and reliable and therefore we should have confidence in his word.

Joshua 21:45 (KJV) There failed not ought of any good thing which the LORD had spoken unto the house of Israel; all came to pass.

God cannot fail; hence, you can put your trust in his word, and that was exactly what Joshua did and the scripture says not one of the promises that the Lord made to Joshua failed. So also, I prophesy to you the reader of this book, that as you put your confidence in the Lord, every good and perfect promise of God for your life will come to pass in Jesus name, amen.

2 Kings 18:5 (KJV) He trusted in the LORD God of Israel; so that after him was none like him among all the kings of Judah, nor *any* that were before him.

2 Kings 18:6-7 (KJV) For he clave to the LORD, *and* departed not from following him, but kept his commandments, which the LORD commanded Moses. And the LORD was with him; *and* he prospered whithersoever he went forth: and he rebelled against the king of Assyria, and served him not.

To cleave to something implies that you have confidence in that thing to support you or even save you in times of need. King Hezekiah clave to Jehovah and he prospered wherever he went. Brethren, God is dependable; if you put your trust in him, prosperity in all areas shall be your testimony in Jesus name, amen.

2. BELIEVE IN GOD

Confidence in God will also make you to believe him, if you do not believe that somebody have the ability to save you in times of need, you would not want to put your confidence in him.

Philippians 1:6 (KJV) Being confident of this very thing, that he which hath begun a good work in you will perform *it* until the day of Jesus Christ:

When Paul the Apostle found himself in crisis during a storm at the sea in **Acts 27** and it appeared that all were doomed to perish at the sea, an angel appeared to him and told him that he was not going to perish and that he must appear before Caesar, and that God had given him the lives of those who sailed with him. He believed the word of the Lord.

Acts 27:25 (KJV) Wherefore, sirs, be of good cheer: for I believe God, that it shall be even as it was told me.

Therefore, for you to have confidence in God, you must believe the scriptures as the word of God, that his word is true and can be relied on, that he will do what he says he will do.

Numbers 23:19 (KJV) God *is* not a man, that he should lie; neither the son of man, that he should repent: hath he said, and shall he not do *it*? or hath he spoken, and shall he not make it good?

3. FEAR OF GOD

Fear of God also produces confidence. **Proverbs 14:26 (KJV)** In the fear of the LORD *is* strong confidence: and his children shall have a place of refuge.

Anyone who claims the promises of God and does not fear him cannot have the faith in God that produces confidence in Him that God will keep his word.

Genesis 39:9 (KJV) *There is* none greater in this house than I; neither hath he kept back any thing from me but thee, because thou *art* his wife: how then can I do this great wickedness, and sin against God?

Joseph did not just claim the promises of God but demonstrated that he had confidence in God by fearing him when the enemy dangled temptation to him. Brethren, for us to demonstrate we have confidence in God, you must show that you fear God.

HOW TO DEMONSTRATE CONFIDENCE IN YOUR GOD

Boldness:

This is holy boldness that every child of God should have, this boldness comes from knowing God:

Acts 4:13 (KJV) Now when they saw the boldness of Peter and John, and perceived that they were unlearned and ignorant men, they marvelled; and they took knowledge of them, that they had been with Jesus.

When you look at the Bible, believers who had confidence in God demonstrated great boldness.

Daniel 3:16-18 (KJV) Shadrach, Meshach, and Abed-nego, answered and said to the king, O Nebuchadnezzar, **we *are* not careful to answer thee in this matter. If it be *so*, our God whom we serve is able to deliver us from the burning fiery furnace, and he will deliver *us* out of thine hand, O king.** But if not, be it known unto thee, O king, that we will not serve thy gods, nor worship the golden image which thou hast set up.

That is great confidence on the part of Shadrach, Meshach and Abed – nego, for them to say we are not careful to answer you the king in this matter, they were faced with fiery furnace and yet they could demonstrate such confidence in God because they knew whom they believed.

2 Timothy 1:12 (KJV) For the which cause I also suffer these things: nevertheless I am not ashamed: for I know whom I have believed, and am persuaded that he is able to keep that which I have committed unto him against that day.

Hebrews 13:5-6 (KJV) Let your conversation be without covetousness; and be content with such things that you have: for he hath said, I will never leave thee, nor forsake thee. So that we may boldly say, The Lord *is* my helper, and I will not fear what man shall do unto me.

MANY PEOPLE DEMONSTRATE CONFIDENCE IN THE FOLLOWING

Money / Gold:

Job 31:24 (KJV) If I have made gold my hope, or have said to the fine gold, *Thou art* my confidence;

Job said I have not made gold my confidence. If I had made gold my confidence, then I would have been entitled to be punished; the reason for the punishment will be because I have denied God that is above, that he is the source of the blessing.

Job 31:28 (KJV) This also *were* an iniquity *to be punished by* the judge: for I should have denied the God *that is* above.

Talents:

While talents and gifts are good and could promote a man. Care had to be taken that it does not turn to something else that replaces God in our lives.

Acts 12:21-23 (KJV) And upon a set day Herod, arrayed in royal apparel, sat upon his throne, and made an oration unto them.

And the people gave a shout, *saying, It is* the voice of a god, and not of a man. And immediately the angel of the Lord smote him, because he gave not God the glory: and he was eaten of worms, and gave up the ghost.

Herod was a gifted speaker, he had oratory gift and he spoke on a particular day, instead of him and the people to give glory to God, the giver of all good things, he allowed pride to come in and he received great judgment for his sin.

Confidence in Self:

While self-confidence is good, confidence in self without God could be a sin and could spell failure.

Judges 16:20 (KJV) And she said, The Philistines *be* upon thee, Samson. And he awoke out of his sleep, and said, I will go out as at other times before, and shake myself. And he wist not that the LORD was departed from him.

Samson was anointed and he could bring down anything on his way, that gave him confidence in himself, as time went on Samson started living carelessly and he began to put more confidence in the gift rather than the giver and that spelled his doom.

Confidence in God:

Brethren, God does not want us to put our confidence in any other thing but himself alone. Paul the Apostle said in **Philippians 3:3 (KJV)** For we are the circumcision, which worship God in the spirit, and rejoice in Christ Jesus, and have no confidence in the flesh.

God wants us his children to put our confidence in him and that he will fight our battles.

Psalm 27:3 (KJV) Though an host should encamp against me, my heart shall not fear: though war should rise against me, in this *will* I *be* confident.

HOW DO I DEVELOP CONFIDENCE IN GOD?

1. Confidence in God starts with Salvation:

The psalmist is confident that whatever comes his way, that the Lord his salvation will hide and protect him from all danger, then why should I tremble (Psalms 27:1). The three Hebrew children also said the same thing, we know our God is able to deliver us. It takes a man who knows the God he serves to make such a bold pronouncement. Knowing God gives boldness, the bible says that one of the inheritances of a righteous man is boldness (confidence).

Proverbs 28:1 (KJV) The wicked flee when no man pursueth: but the righteous are bold as a lion.

Ephesians 3:12 (KJV) In whom we have boldness and access with confidence by the faith of him.

2. Confidence Could be Progressive:

After knowing God, then, confidence in God could further be developed even after salvation or knowing God. David; before he faced Goliath, he had been confronted with lion and bear while taken care of his father's sheep and therefore when faced later with Goliath, because he had defeated lion and bear in the wilderness, he was confident that God would also bring down Goliath for him. His confidence was more in God than in himself.

1 Samuel 17:37 (KJV) David said moreover, The LORD that delivered me out of the paw of the lion, and out of the paw of the bear, he will deliver me out of the hand of this Philistine. And Saul said unto David, Go, and the LORD be with thee.

If you have not trusted God for anything before now, then it is almost impossible to trust God for something bigger. Someone asked the renowned evangelist, Billy Graham, that she was scheduled to attend a surgery for a disease, and she asked Billy Graham to know if she should attend the surgery or not. Billy Graham retorted using David as an example that before David faced the test of his life in the case of Goliath, he had trusted God with lion and bear. Therefore, if you have not believed God for mundane and small matter or even small sickness like headache, then it will be wise that you heed the advice of your doctor by going for the surgery, this is because confidence in God is progressive.

3. Holy Spirit Gives Confidence:

Holy Ghost gives confidence, this is because if you have the Holy Ghost, you have God within you, then it is difficult for such a person to be gripped by the power of fear.

At one point in lives of the apostles, they asked Jesus for increased faith, what they were saying to Jesus in essence was we want to have more confidence in God. For instance, at the time when Jesus was arrested and going through interrogation, Peter denied Jesus three (3) times because he was paralysed with fear. However, after he and other brethren received the Holy Ghost in Acts 2: 1-4 and healed a crippled man that laid at the beautiful gate. Peter and John were brought before the council and they were asked by what power did they make the crippled man well.**Acts 4:8-10 (KJV)** Then Peter, filled with the Holy Ghost, said unto them, Ye rulers of the people, and elders of Israel, If we this day be examined of the good deed done to the impotent man, by what means he is made whole; Be it known unto you all, and to all the people of Israel, that by the name of Jesus Christ of Nazareth, whom ye crucified, whom God raised from the dead, *even* by him doth this man stand here before you whole.

Peter was not hesitant or afraid to tell the council the truth of the word of God, this is because in Acts 2 he had been changed to a different man by the power of the Holy Ghost.

Acts 4:13 (KJV) Now when they saw the boldness of Peter and John, and perceived that they were unlearned and ignorant men, they marvelled; and they took knowledge of them, that they had been with Jesus.

4. Move With Faith Filled People:

Confidence could also be contagious, that a company of sheep being led by lion can defeat a company of lion being led by a sheep. This is because, the man in the front filled with faith and confidence, could rub his faith and confidence on the other members of the team.

Proverbs 27:17 (KJV) Iron sharpeneth iron; so a man sharpeneth the countenance of his friend.

That is why after David had defeated Goliath, David's brother, Shimea, knowing fully well that David had defeated a giant before, also attempted and defeated another giant, having seen the example of David.

1 Chronicles 20:6-7 (KJV) And yet again there was war at Gath, where was a man of *great* stature, whose fingers and toes *were* four and twenty, six *on each hand*, and six *on each foot*: and he also was the son of the giant. But when he defied Israel, Jonathan the son of Shimea David's brother slew him.

Therefore, for you to have confidence in God to become amazing you, hang out with people that can strengthen your faith in God, not those who discourage or sow seed of doubt and unbelief in your heart. As you do this, amazing breakthroughs shall be your portion in Jesus name, amen. I cannot wait to hear your testimony because it shall surely come!

Chapter EIGHT

REWARD OF OBEDIENCE

Everyone desires to have amazing testimonies and in fact God is prepared to bless everyone that is a child of the living God with amazing testimonies.

Isaiah 45:19 (KJV) I have not spoken in secret, in a dark place of the earth: I said not unto the seed of Jacob, Seek ye me in vain: I the LORD speak righteousness, I declare things that are right.

God is ever ready to bless us as his children with all the good things of life that we desire.

3 John 2 (KJV) Beloved, I wish above all things that thou mayest prosper and be in health, even as thy soul prospereth.

Though God is desirous of blessing us, many a time we rob ourselves of the blessings of God through disobedience. A child of God that is desirous of God's abundant blessings must avoid like a plague, the "cancer" called disobedience.

Isaiah 1:19-20 (KJV) If ye be willing and obedient, ye shall eat the good of the land: But if ye refuse and rebel, ye shall be devoured with the sword: for the mouth of the LORD hath spoken *it*.

One thing God does not joke with is his word, he even exalts his word above his name. However, believers engage in half obedience and think God does not know. Some believers cherry pick God's words that they are prepared to obey and hence, rob themselves of the blessings of God. Believers who engage with half obedience are put together with the wicked because they pretend to obey God's word while the truth of the matter is that they are walking in disobedience. Half obedience is nothing but disobedience.

Psalms 50:16 (NLT) But God says to the wicked: Why bother reciting my decrees and pretending to obey my covenant?

The above passage talked about pretending to obey the word of the Lord, that was exactly what Ananias and Sapphira did in Acts 5:2 when they sold their land and brought part of the money to the Apostles, claiming it was the full amount. With his wife's consent, he kept the rest. This couple, even though they attempted to make some sacrifice for kingdom of God in the early church, their sacrifice was a pretence as they lied to Apostle Peter and they both paid dearly with their lives. Half obedience is no obedience at all, so please be careful to go all the way in obeying the Lord in order for you to enjoy the fulness of the blessings of God.

Believers who obey the word of God do the following:

1. OBEY WHOLEHEARTEDLY

Deuteronomy 26:16 (NLT) Today the Lord your God has commended you to obey all these decrees and regulations. So be careful to obey them wholeheartedly

Once a believer begins to cheery pick which of the counsel or the word of the Lord to obey, then such believer is treading on a dangerous path and the end result will be missing out in the blessings of God. That was the mistake of Saul; God told him through Prophet Samuel to destroy all the Amalekites without sparing men, women, children, babies, cattle, sheep, goats, camels, and donkeys (1Samuel 15:3) Instead of Saul to completely obey the command of the Lord, he chose to spare Agag, king of the Amalekites, and also spared some of the best sheep and cattle etc. The scripture says that they destroyed only what was worthless or poor quality and kept everything else that appealed to them. This represents an act of disobedience before the Lord, though Saul destroyed some of the men, women, animals etc but his obedience was incomplete and hence, Saul robbed himself of the testimony of the Lord; his kingdom was given to someone else.

1 Samuel 15:28 (KJV) And Samuel said unto him, The LORD hath rent the kingdom of Israel from thee this day, and hath given it to a neighbour of thine, *that is* better than thou.

2. OBEY SINGLE-MINDEDLY

To be single- minded is to be focused. It is to set your affection on something. In the case of the believer, to be single minded is to have only one desire and that is to please the Lord, who died for his sin.

> **2 Timothy 2:4 (KJV)** No man that warreth entangleth himself with the affairs of *this* life; that he may please him who hath chosen him to be a soldier.

Once your heart desire is to please the Lord, then every action of yours will be perfect before the lord.

2 Kings 20:3 (KJV) I beseech thee, O LORD, remember now how I have walked before thee in truth and with a perfect heart, and have done *that which is* good in thy sight. And Hezekiah wept sore.

King Hezekiah had the audacity to challenge God about God's judgement because he evaluated himself in the light of God's word. He was invariably saying father, please look at me, I have walked before you in truth, that is, I have kept thy word, not only in truth, I have also walked with you with a perfect heart. What that means is that look Lord I have walked with you with singleness of heart. I have not been disobedient to your word; I have only done what pleases you. Therefore, God had to revert his decision of untimely death for king Hezekiah.

2 Kings 20:5 (KJV) Turn again, and tell Hezekiah the captain of my people, Thus saith the LORD, the God of David thy father, I have heard thy prayer, I have seen thy tears: behold, I will heal thee: on the third day thou shalt go up unto the house of the LORD.

Hezekiah's perfect heart; coupled with his obedience and faithfulness to the Lord was what brought him his testimony. Child of God, if you are desirous of amazing testimony, one thing you cannot play with his complete obedience.

Let us now look at God's promises to those who are obedient to him. God promises amazing blessings for the obedient. Some of the blessings include:

1. Success and Prosperity:

Psalm 112:1-3 (KJV) Praise ye the LORD. Blessed *is* the man *that* feareth the LORD, *that* delighteth greatly in his commandments. His seed shall be mighty upon earth: the generation of the upright shall be blessed. Wealth and riches *shall be* in his house: and his righteousness endureth forever.

Child of God, please look at the amazing promise of God for those who fear the Lord and those who greatly delight in his commandments, not only did God promise to bless them, even their children and their children's children shall be mighty upon the earth. This tells me that God is not only happy to bless the believer, but even generations after him have God's blessings extended to them as long as they walk in the path of obedience.

Deuteronomy 4:40 (NLT) if you obey all the decrees and commands, I am giving you today, all will be well with you and your children.

The promise above is awesome, no one can make such a promise except the Almighty God.

Psalms 132:11-12 The Lord swore an oath to David with a promise he will never take back: I will place one of your descendants on your throne. If your descendants obey the terms of my covenant.

If you want a glorious testimony for yourself and for your children and generations after you, please walk in truth and obedience to the word of God and this shall be your testimony in Jesus name, amen.

God spoke to Isaac saying ''I will not withhold my blessings upon your life and generations after just because your father Abraham obeyed my voice".

Genesis 26:4-5 (KJV) And I will make thy seed to multiply as the stars of heaven, and will give unto thy seed all these countries; and in thy seed shall all the nations of the earth be blessed; Because that Abraham obeyed my voice, and kept my charge, my commandments, my statutes, and my laws.

No wonder God's blessings continued to Isaac and also manifested in the life of Jacob.

Genesis 26:12-13 (KJV) Then Isaac sowed in that land, and received in the same year an hundredfold: and the LORD blessed him. And the man waxed great, and went forward, and grew until he became very great:

JACOB:

Genesis 30:43 (KJV) And the man increased exceedingly, and had much cattle, and maidservants, and menservants, and camels, and asses.

I pray for you today, that God's blessings will not stop with you but shall extend to generations after you as you and your children walk in obedience in Jesus name, amen.

2. Seasonal Rains:

Leviticus 26:3-5 (KJV) If ye walk in my statutes, and keep my commandments, and do them; Then I will give you rain in due season, and the land shall yield her increase, and the trees of the field shall yield their fruit. And your threshing shall reach unto the vintage, and the vintage shall reach unto the sowing time: and ye shall eat your bread to the full, and dwell in your land safely.

Rain is important for anything that is planted to grow and produce harvest. Hence, when there is no rain, there is famine like in the days of Elijah. Many people believe in hard work, however, as important as it is to work hard, it is equally important for your work to be blessed by God.

Psalm 127:1-2 (KJV) A Song of degrees for Solomon. Except the LORD build the house, they labour in vain that build it: except the LORD keep the city, the watchman waketh *but* in vain. *It is* vain for you to rise up early, to sit up late, to eat the bread of sorrows: *for* so he giveth his beloved sleep.

Not every hard worker has something to show for his hard work.

Haggai 1:9 (KJV) Ye looked for much, and, lo, *it came* to little; and when ye brought *it* home, I did blow upon it. Why? saith the LORD of hosts. Because of mine house that *is* waste, and ye run every man unto his own house.

Child of God, there is just one thing that guarantees blessings of God on your life and business. That thing is obedience, so if you are determined to walk in full obedience to the word of God then you are set for amazing blessings and testimonies.

3. Special Treasure:

Exodus 19:5 (KJV) Now therefore, if ye will obey my voice indeed, and keep my covenant, then ye shall be a peculiar treasure unto me above all people: for all the earth *is* mine:

A treasure is something that is valuable, God is saying if you obey my voice, then you shall be a peculiar treasure unto me above all the people. In essence, God is assuring you that you will become valuable in his sight. There are few people in the scriptures that God calls treasure. One of them is Moses:

Numbers 12:7 (KJV) My servant Moses *is* not so, who *is* faithful in all mine house.

To be faithful is to walk in obedience. A treasure is also something that you find difficult to do without and that you are prepared to use for great task.

2 Timothy 2:21 (KJV) If a man therefore purge himself from these, he shall be a vessel unto honour, sanctified, and meet for the master's use, *and* prepared unto every good work.

Therefore, anyone that desires to be used of God must strive to walk in complete obedience and that is when the power of God can come upon such individual.

Some fail in their assignment because of disobedience:

> **Numbers 20:12 (KJV)** And the LORD spake unto Moses and Aaron, Because ye believed me not, to sanctify me in the eyes of the children of Israel, therefore ye shall not bring this congregation into the land which I have given them.

Moses could not take the people of God into the promise land just because of one single act of disobedience, so be careful child of God.

4. Enemy to your Enemy:

There is no betraying the fact that everyone that aspires to achieve one great thing or the other face opposition. Even Jesus Christ our Lord had great opposition in his ministry.

Luke 6:7 (KJV) And the scribes and Pharisees watched him, whether he would heal on the sabbath day; that they might find an accusation against him.

Jesus was confronted several times in his ministry by opposing forces. In fact, that was the reason he was crucified because the scribes and Pharisees were envious of him and they became his enemy.

Matthew 27:12 (KJV) And when he was accused of the chief priests and elders, he answered nothing.

Matthew 27:18 (KJV) For he knew that for envy they had delivered him.

If Jesus the son of God could face opposition in his ministry, whatever you desire to achieve, you should also expect opposition. This is because the enemy will raise opposition in order to stop your testimony. Therefore, it is better to have God on your side so that you can overcome the wicked one.

Exodus 23:22 (KJV) But if thou shalt indeed obey his voice and do all that I speak; then I will be an enemy unto thine enemies, and an adversary unto thine adversaries.

That scripture is saying God wants to fight your battles, God is saying, please let me by doing all that I command you. If you do the opposite, then you are treading on the path of losing to the kingdom of darkness. Obedience is what guarantee your victory. So please walk in obedience!

Chapter NINE

AMAZING TESTIMONIES THROUGH OBEDIENCE

When God decide to bless a believer, he examines his heart to know the state of his heart, whether he will do his will or not. **Ecclesiastes 10: 5-6 (NLT)** There is another evil I have seen under the sun. Kings and rulers make a grave mistake when they give great authority to foolish people and low positions to people of proven worth. Man may make mistake of committing great responsibility to an individual without proving them, because it is impossible for man to know the thought of another man except the Spirit of the Lord reveals it.

In the case of Almighty God, it is different, God examines the hearts and reins of men. **Jeremiah 17:10 (KJV)** I the LORD search the heart, *I* try the reins, even to give every man according to his ways, *and* according to the fruit of his doings. Therefore, before God will lift you to higher level, he will test your heart. Even Jesus the Son of God was examined before he was lifted and given a name that is above every other name.

Mathew 4:1 (AMPC) Then Jesus was led (guided) by the Holy Spirit into the wilderness (desert) to be tempted (tested and tried) by the devil.

Jesus was tempted by three P's of life (Performance, Possession and Popularity) and he passed the tests. He said in Mathew 4:10 (ESV) Begone, Satan! For it has been written, You shall worship the Lord your God and Him alone shall you serve. Jesus passed the performance test that he should convert a stone to bread. The enemy told him that for you to prove that you the Son of God, so that all would believe you, you must perform that miracle. Jesus did not need to prove that he was the Son of God, he knew his identity. He rejected the offer of the devil and thus passed the test resoundingly.

He also passed the possession test, the devil promised him the whole world if he could only but bow down to him. Jesus rejected this offer as well and lastly, the enemy dangled the bait of popularity before him and said if he could jump down from the pinnacle of the temple that would prove that he was the son of God; he also passed this final test. The scripture says in **Philippians 2:8-9 (KJV)** And being found in fashion as a man, he humbled himself, and became obedient unto death, even the death of the cross. Wherefore God also hath highly exalted him, and given him a name which is above every name.

As you can see in the life of Jesus, he was not lifted without a test, he passed all the tests that God put him through in the hands of the devil before he experienced God's lifting.

What of Abraham? A man that is called the friend of God:

> **James 2:23 (KJV)** And the scripture was fulfilled which saith, Abraham believed God, and it was imputed unto him for righteousness: and he was called the Friend of God.
>
> **2 Chronicles 20:7 (KJV)** *Art* not thou our God, *who* didst drive out the inhabitants of this land before thy people Israel, and gavest it to the seed of Abraham thy friend forever?

Before God called Abraham his friend, God tested Abraham's faithfulness and Loyalty. God asked for his only child, the one he loved, the child of promise.

Genesis 22:1-2 (KJV) And it came to pass after these things, that God did tempt Abraham, and said unto him, Abraham: and he said, Behold, *here* I *am*. And he said, Take now thy son, thine only *son* Isaac, whom thou lovest, and get thee into the land of Moriah; and offer him there for a burnt offering upon one of the mountains which I will tell thee of.

The word tempted in the above verse like I said earlier on could easily be translated or replaced with proved, tried or tested. Abraham passed the test as he did not hesitate to obey the instruction of the Lord.

Genesis 22:3 (KJV) And Abraham rose up early in the morning, and saddled his ass, and took two of his young men with him, and Isaac his son, and clave the wood for the burnt offering, and rose up, and went unto the place of which God had told him.

Abraham was prepared to sacrifice his only son as instructed by God. Therefore, God said to Abraham, now I know that you fear me and swore an oath to Abraham saying "in blessing I will bless you and in multiplying I will multiply you because you did not withhold your only son from me".

Genesis 22:12 (KJV) And he said, Lay not thine hand upon the lad, neither do thou any thing unto him: for now I know that thou fearest God, seeing thou hast not withheld thy son, thine only *son* from me.

Genesis 22:16-18 (KJV) And said, By myself have I sworn, saith the LORD, for because thou hast done this thing, and hast not withheld thy son, thine only *son*: That in blessing I will bless thee, and in multiplying I will multiply thy seed as the stars of the heaven, and as the sand which *is* upon the sea shore; and thy seed shall possess the gate of his enemies; And in thy seed shall all the nations of the earth be blessed; because thou hast obeyed my voice.

Abraham passed the test before he qualified for the blessings of God.

Joseph experienced the lifting of God also but not without a test:

> **Psalm 105:18-19 (KJV)** Whose feet they hurt with fetters: he was laid in iron: Until the time that his word came: the word of the LORD tried him.

Before Joseph found himself in the palace, he was lied against, he was sent to the prison and he was even sold as slaves by his brothers and yet he did not sin against God. That is passing the tests.

Psalm 105:20-22 (KJV) The king sent and loosed him; *even* the ruler of the people, and let him go free. He made him lord of his house, and ruler of all his substance: To bind his princes at his pleasure; and teach his senators wisdom.

After passing God's tests, he was ready for a higher office by becoming second to Pharaoh. I pray that you also after passing through the test God would find you worthy for his promotion in Jesus name, Amen.

Why do we have to get tested before amazing testimony?

1. TO PROVE WHAT IS IN THE HEART

God allows his children to go through some tough times as test in order to know the true state of their hearts.

Deuteronomy 8:2 (KJV) And thou shalt remember all the way which the LORD thy God led thee these forty years in the wilderness, to humble thee, *and* to prove thee, to know what *was* in thine heart, whether thou wouldest keep his commandments, or no.

Joseph went through temptation by Potiphar's wife and he refused to yield to the pressure from this adulterous woman. He could have compromised but he refused thus showing that his heart was right with God.

2. TO DEVELOP CHARACTER

Psalm 66:10-12 (KJV) For thou, O God, hast proved us: thou hast tried us, as silver is tried. Thou broughtest us into the net; thou laidst affliction upon our loins. Thou hast caused men to ride over our heads; we went through fire and through water: but thou broughtest us out into a wealthy *place*.

Before glory becomes manifest, God takes the believer through the furnace of affliction in order to develop the character of the believer. Daniel, Shadrach, Meshach and Abed-nego, Joseph, name them, they all went through all their tough times and eventually God brought them out of affliction and brought them to their wealthy place.

Gold is first tried and will have to go through fire before it becomes a valuable substance of great price!

Job 23:10 (KJV) But he knoweth the way that I take: *when* he hath tried me, I shall come forth as gold.

3. TO KNOW THE GENUINENESS OF YOUR FAITH

1 Peter 1:7(AMPC) So that (the genuineness) of your faith may be tested (your faith) which is infinitely more precious than the perishable gold which is tested and purified by fire.(This proving of your faith is intended) to redound to (your) praise and glory and honour when Jesus Christ (the Messiah, the Anointed One) is revealed.

To prove the genuineness of any precious metal, experts always pass it through fire to determine if such metal is genuine or fake. God does the same to prove if we are going to buck under pressure or not. That was Job's experience, the enemy said to God, Job only feared you because of the fact that you have blessed him, remove his protection and he will curse you to your face.

Job 1:11 (KJV) But put forth thine hand now, and touch all that he hath, and he will curse thee to thy face.

Job proved to be a dependable and reliable child of God and he did not deny the God of his salvation.

Job 13:15 (KJV) Though he slay me, yet will I trust in him: but I will maintain mine own ways before him.

Job passed the test and God lifted him and gave him double of that which he had before:

Job 42:10 (KJV) And the LORD turned the captivity of Job, when he prayed for his friends: also the LORD gave Job twice as much as he had before.

I pray that you also will endure whatever temptation and challenges you are going through right now. I know that by the time you pass the test, amazing testimonies shall be your portion in Jesus name, amen

Please never give up, let us patiently wait for the promise of God; for we shall reap if we faint not.

Galatians 6:9 (KJV) And let us not be weary in well doing: for in due season we shall reap, if we faint not.

Our reward is not only earthly but also heavenly, even after we pass the test of this life, God has promised the crown of life to as many that endure temptation, pass the test and be eventually approved.

James 1:12 (KJV) Blessed *is* the man that endureth temptation: for when he is tried, he shall receive the crown of life, which the Lord hath promised to them that love him.

Chapter
TEN

MIND OF CHRIST NECESSARY FOR AMAZING TESTIMONIES

Amazing testimonies is the inheritance of every child of God, however, for the believer to appropriate these testimonies, the believer has to have the mind of Christ. The reason for this is that many a time, a believer is confronted with challenges that when you look at it from the carnal or fleshly perspective, you might conclude that there is no way out. For instance, at the Red Sea the children of Israel were faced with Red Sea in front of them and Pharaoh's army was fast approaching. Ordinarily, when you look at that scenario, you would conclude that there is no escape for the children of Israel, that they are all either killed or perished at the sea. Moses, having a different mind declared to the children of Israel that they should move forward despite that he could also see Red Sea in front. He declared that they should move forward, and they shall see the salvation of God today. Moses's mind was definitely different from the rest of the people.

The mind is the place you do the following:

1. Engage in thoughts with the world around you:

Proverbs 23:7 (KJV) For as he thinketh in his heart, so *is* he: Eat and drink, saith he to thee; but his heart *is* not with thee.

The bible in Isaiah 55:8 (NLT) says that my thoughts are nothing like your thoughts. It is in your mind, that thoughts take place, and it is what you think about that determines what you do. It is through what you do that you engage with the world

2. Reasoning:

Luke 5:22 (KJV) But when Jesus perceived their thoughts, he answering said unto them, What reason ye in your hearts?

The mind is a place we reason issues out and therefore it is important we guide our hearts diligently because out of it comes the issues of life.

3. Attitudes to life are developed:

Philippians 2:5-6 (KJV) Let this mind be in you, which was also in Christ Jesus: Who, being in the form of God, thought it not robbery to be equal with God:

When you read the above passage in NLT version, mind is replaced with attitude. All the attitudes we put up in life emanate from the mind, whether positive or negative.

When you read the bible, both the minds and hearts are used inter-changeably. The mind and heart of man represent our inner being which is what describes who we truly are. The mind determines the course of our lives either as believer or unbeliever.

Proverbs 4:23 (KJV) Keep thy heart with all diligence; for out of it *are* the issues of life.

Whatever you allow to permeate your heart and mind determine the course of your life.

Then Pharaoh will think, the Israelites are confused and they are trapped in the wilderness and he will chase after the Israelites Exodus 14:3-4. Why will Pharaoh chase after them? The reason he would chase after them was the thought he allowed to prevail in his heart.

Numbers 13:31-33 (KJV) But the men that went up with him said, We be not able to go up against the people; for they *are* stronger than we. And they brought up an evil report of the land which they had searched unto the children of Israel, saying, The land, through which we have gone to search it, *is* a land that eateth up the inhabitants thereof; and all the people that we saw in it *are* men of a great stature. And there we saw the giants, the sons of Anak, *which come* of the giants: and we were in our own sight as grasshoppers, and so we were in their sight.

The Israelites had seen mighty hands of God in Egypt and even at the Red Sea yet they allowed self-limiting thoughts to permeate their hearts and therefore many of them could not get to the promise land, not because God could not get them there but their thoughts prevented them from seeing the land the Lord their God promised them.

I remember when we were pursuing the idea of purchasing our church building, some members of the church were saying among themselves, how many are we that we are pursuing the purchase of a church building? Some were saying where are we going to get enough money to purchase the building? All these statements are coming from the minds that look at current situation to determine the course of action to take. If I had allowed that to take root in my mind, we would not be a proud owner of a church building today.

CHARACTERISTICS OF A NATURAL MAN:

1. A natural man sets his mind on things of the flesh:

Romans 8:5 (KJV) For they that are after the flesh do mind the things of the flesh; but they that are after the Spirit the things of the Spirit.

Therefore, a natural man finds it difficult to understand the things of the Spirit. They will always look at things from perspective of what they can see or hear. Therefore, it is almost impossible for such to experience amazing testimonies.

Ephesians 4:17-18 (KJV) This I say therefore, and testify in the Lord, that ye henceforth walk not as other Gentiles walk, in the vanity of their mind, Having the understanding darkened, being alienated from the life of God through the ignorance that is in them, because of the blindness of their heart:

2. A Natural man's heart is hostile to God: An unregenerate heart is an enemy of God. He cannot trust God nor can he please God.

Romans 8:7-8 (KJV) Because the carnal mind *is* enmity against God: for it is not subject to the law of God, neither indeed can be. So then they that are in the flesh cannot please God.

3. A Natural man's heart is Controlled by fleshly desires:

Romans 8:6 (KJV) For to be carnally minded *is* death; but to be spiritually minded *is* life and peace.

To be carnally minded is to be controlled by desires of the flesh. What a natural man does is to look for what is comfortable to the flesh and therefore it is impossible to be controlled by the flesh and still have the mind of Christ. Those who are in the flesh do not have the mind of Christ.

To develop the mind of Christ, a man has to come to the saviour. That is, a natural man must come to the knowledge of the Son of God. Every unbeliever has a veil covering his eyes and therefore cannot comprehend or understand the things of God.

Ephesians 4:17-18 (KJV) This I say therefore, and testify in the Lord, that ye henceforth walk not as other Gentiles walk, in the vanity of their mind, Having the understanding darkened, being alienated from the life of God through the ignorance that is in them, because of the blindness of their heart:

The prophet Isaiah said the eyes of the unbeliever are plastered over so they cannot see, and their minds closed so they cannot understand **(Isaiah 44:18-NIV).**

2 Corinthians 4:4 (KJV) In whom the god of this world hath blinded the minds of them which believe not, lest the light of the glorious gospel of Christ, who is the image of God, should shine unto them.

You might be wondering, how then can the unbeliever whose heart and mind have been plastered or covered by the devil see the glorious gospel of Christ that has power to liberate and set free.

2 Corinthians 3:16 (KJV) Nevertheless when it shall turn to the Lord, the vail shall be taken away.

The above passage states that that covering that the enemy blinds people with so that they cannot see the glorious liberty that is in Christ Jesus can only be taken away by turning to the Lord, that is by turning to Christ Jesus. It is in Christ that you receive a new heart and mind.

Isaiah 55:7 (KJV) Let the wicked forsake his way, and the unrighteous man his thoughts: and let him return unto the LORD, and he will have mercy upon him; and to our God, for he will abundantly pardon.

It is when you come to the Lord, that a supernatural exchange takes place. He takes away your former heart of stone and gives you a new heart of flesh and that is when your hearts and minds are opened. It is like a computer software that has been corrupted and could not function at its optimal level anymore because of many viruses.

Ezekiel 36:26 (KJV) A new heart also will I give you, and a new spirit will I put within you: and I will take away the stony heart out of your flesh, and I will give you a new heart of flesh.

When you receive a new heart and mind, the way you think begin to change. You begin to see the scriptures not as just letters but as the revelation of the mind of God to those that believe.

Romans 12:2 (KJV) And be not conformed to this world: but be ye transformed by the renewing of your mind, that ye may prove what *is* that good, and acceptable, and perfect, will of God.

Romans 12:2 (NLT) Don't copy the behaviour and customs of this world, but let God transform you into a new person by changing the way you think. Then you will learn to know God's will for you, which is good and pleasing and perfect.

A believer, that is a man that is born again having confessed, repented, and surrendered his life to Christ is a candidate for amazing testimonies. Why is this so? The reason is simple, a believer then believes the word of God is true and powerful and that word would accomplish what God says.

Hebrews 4:12 (KJV) For the word of God *is* quick, and powerful, and sharper than any two-edged sword, piercing even to the dividing asunder of soul and spirit, and of the joints and marrow, and *is* a discerner of the thoughts and intents of the heart.

A believer then puts his faith in the word of God. He believes that the word of God is the final authority on all issues of life. He puts his confidence in ever living word of God.

Isaiah 40:8 (KJV) The grass withereth, the flower fadeth: but the word of our God shall stand forever.

1 Peter 1:23 (KJV) Being born again, not of corruptible seed, but of incorruptible, by the word of God, which liveth and abideth forever.

Please note that the mere fact that you have surrendered your heart to the Lord does not mean that the enemy, the devil, will go to sleep and not trouble you any longer. Your heart and mind continue to be a battle ground for the enemy and the Holy Spirit. The one you yield your heart to then becomes your master. However, the scripture admonishes not to give room to the devil in our hearts.

Ephesians 4:27 (KJV) Neither give place to the devil.

Romans 6:16 (KJV) Know ye not, that to whom ye yield yourselves servants to obey, his servants ye are to whom ye obey, whether of sin unto death, or of obedience unto righteousness?

Therefore, in order to live the new life, you now have in Christ Jesus, you must develop your new mind. That is what is called developing the mind of Christ.

HOW THEN DO YOU DEVELOP THE MIND OF CHRIST?

1. Train your mind:

Every athlete trains his mind, even those who are paid millions of dollars have coaches and psychologists who train their minds before a competition commences. You also for you to have a successful Christian life filled with amazing testimonies, you must train your mind. The mind is a battle ground, the enemy will want to drop so many dirty things in your mind, but you must steadfastly resist him.

1 Peter 5:9 (KJV) Whom resist stedfast in the faith, knowing that the same afflictions are accomplished in your brethren that are in the world.

You must bring every rebellious thought in obedience to the word of God. That is the weapon you have to fight the good fight of faith. The enemy will bring in false narrative and argument into your mind. The strategy of the enemy is to derail you and make sure you lose your testimony, you must however stand your ground resolutely and that testimony you desire shall be yours in Jesus name, amen.

2 Corinthians 10:3-5 (KJV) For though we walk in the flesh, we do not war after the flesh: (For the weapons of our warfare *are* not carnal, but mighty through God to the pulling down of strong holds;) Casting down imaginations, and every high thing that exalteth itself against the knowledge of God, and bringing into captivity every thought to the obedience of Christ;

2. Discipline your mind:

Without a disciplined mind you are bound to lose the battle against the enemy. Remember the story of David in **2 Samuel 11:2 (KJV)** And it came to pass in an eveningtide, that David arose from off his bed, and walked upon the roof of the king's house: and from the roof he saw a woman washing herself; and the woman *was* very beautiful to look upon.

David went into sin because he could not discipline his mind not to look at objects that would put him in sin.

Proverbs 4:23 (KJV) Keep thy heart with all diligence; for out of it *are* the issues of life.

Matthew 15:19 (KJV) For out of the heart proceed evil thoughts, murders, adulteries, fornications, thefts, false witness, blasphemies:

If you want to develop the mid of Christ, you have got to discipline your mind against every darts of the wicked. The enemy will not give up, he will continue to throw negative thoughts into your heart, but you must resist him.

3. Renew your mind:

Renewing your mind is a daily exercise. Like the computer slangs, garbage in garbage out. You must be deliberate by putting the word of God into your heart.

Psalms 49:3-5 (NLT) For my words are wise, and my thoughts are filled with insights. I listen carefully to many proverbs............ why should I fear when troubles come?

It is the word of God that you have stored in your mind that you will draw out in times of trouble. If you do not store in anything then there will be nothing to draw at the time of need.

Psalm 119:97-98 (KJV) MEM. O how love I thy law! it *is* my meditation all the day. Thou through thy commandments hast made me wiser than mine enemies: for they *are* ever with me.

4. Renew your thoughts with the Holy Spirit:

God has given us the Holy Spirit, one of his function is to be with us. When Jesus was leaving the earth, he said I will not leave you without a helper. I will send him unto you and he will forever be with you.

John 14:16 (KJV) And I will pray the Father, and he shall give you another Comforter, that he may abide with you forever;

You cannot develop the mind of Christ without the help of the Holy Spirit.

Titus 3:5-6 (KJV) Not by works of righteousness which we have done, but according to his mercy he saved us, by the washing of regeneration, and renewing of the Holy Ghost; Which he shed on us abundantly through Jesus Christ our Saviour;

As a believer, you have got to ask the Holy Spirit to renew your heart. The word of God through the Holy Spirit has the power to cleanse our heart and mind.

Ephesians 5:26 (KJV) That he might sanctify and cleanse it with the washing of water by the word.

Ephesians 4:23 (KJV) And be renewed in the spirit of your mind.

5. Make Supplication Regularly and consistently:

Nehemiah 4:1-3 (KJV) But it came to pass, that when Sanballat heard that we builded the wall, he was wroth, and took great indignation, and mocked the Jews. And he spake before his brethren and the army of Samaria, and said, What do these feeble Jews? will they fortify themselves? will they sacrifice? will they make an end in a day? will they revive the stones out of the heaps of the rubbish which are burned? Now Tobiah the Ammonite *was* by him, and he said, Even that which they build, if a fox go up, he shall even break down their stone wall.

The mind is battle ground as I stated earlier. The enemy of the Jews having heard that they had commenced the rebuilding of the broken-down wall strategized to stop the work. They knew if they could make them not to believe they could do the work, then they would be able to succeed to stop them from continuing with the work. The enemy of Israelites began to make jest of them, they began to say what do these feeble, poor Jews think they are doing, do they think they can rebuild this wall with just a few sacrifices? These are statement to make them to stop the work and stop their testimony. What did the Jews do as a result of this?

Nehemiah 4:4 (KJV) Hear, O our God; for we are despised: and turn their reproach upon their own head, and give them for a prey in the land of captivity:

They prayed, they committed their ways to the Lord, they prayed for God's help. In times of great difficulty, you too can learn from

Nehemiah in the above scriptures. Pray regularly and consistently that your faith will not fail, and you will see amazing intervention of God in your life in Jesus name, amen.

6. Know the God You Serve:

Daniel 11:32 (KJV) And such as do wickedly against the covenant shall he corrupt by flatteries: but the people that do know their God shall be strong, and do *exploits*.

When you know the God you serve, it helps you not to succumb to the intimidation of the enemy. When Paul and Silas were thrown into prison, instead of feeling discouraged and depressed, they began to sing praises to their God; it takes a man who knows his God to sing at the time of difficulty.

Acts 16:25 (KJV) And at midnight Paul and Silas prayed, and sang praises unto God: and the prisoners heard them.

This is the advice of the Lord to the believer to allow the word of God to dwell in our heart, this word of the Lord could include hymns, songs and praises.

Colossians 3:16 (KJV) Let the word of Christ dwell in you richly in all wisdom; teaching and admonishing one another in psalms and hymns and spiritual songs, singing with grace in your hearts to the Lord.

Ephesians 5:19 (KJV) Speaking to yourselves in psalms and hymns and spiritual songs, singing and making melody in your heart to the Lord.

Lastly, having put to practice the above, you must continually and deliberately put the following into your heart.

Philippians 4:8 (KJV) Finally, brethren, whatsoever things are true, whatsoever things *are* honest, whatsoever things *are* just, whatsoever things *are* pure, whatsoever things *are* lovely, whatsoever things *are* of good report; if *there be* any virtue, and if *there be* any praise, think on these things.

Once you take care of your thought life, then nothing will be impossible for you to achieve, then amazing breakthroughs shall come your way in Jesus name, amen. This is because you serve a God that can do beyond what we think or even imagine.

Ephesians 3:20-21 (KJV) Now unto him that is able to do exceedingly abundantly above all that we ask or think, according to the power that worketh in us, Unto him *be* glory in the church by Christ Jesus throughout all ages, world without end. Amen.

HOW TO OVERCOME DEFEAT

Defeat is common in sports, politics, business etc Any where there is competition, there will always be winners and losers. In life, you do not win every time, that is just the reality of life. Even though as human beings we face defeat sometimes, God does not want us to brood over defeat and remain defeated:

> **Proverbs 24:16 (KJV)** For a just *man* falleth seven times, and riseth up again: but the wicked shall fall into mischief.

Let us examine why people experience defeat so as to avoid these pitfalls:

1. OVER CONFIDENCE

When people have succeeded for quite a number of times, they tend to believe that they have a magic wand for success, they become bloated in their ego and over confident. That was the situation the children of Israel found themselves on their way to the promise land. They had defeated mightier nations before they got to a small town called Ai, then they concluded in their hearts, Ai was no threat to their conquest, and therefore they did not see the need to send a vast army of Israel against them as they were just but a few, Israel suffered catastrophic defeat:

> **Joshua 7:2-3 (KJV)** And Joshua sent men from Jericho to Ai, which *is* beside Beth-aven, on the east side of Beth-el, and spake unto them, saying, Go up and view the country. And the men went up and viewed Ai. And they returned to Joshua, and said unto him, Let not all the people go up; but let about two or three thousand men go up and smite Ai; *and* make not all the people to labour thither; for they *are but* few.

2. LACK OF ADEQUATE PREPARATION

Preparation is bedrock to success, there is no pursuit that will lead to success without adequate preparation. In fact, there is a saying that preparation when mixed with opportunity is what lead to success.

Ezekiel 38:7 (KJV) Be thou prepared, and prepare for thyself, thou, and all thy company that are assembled unto thee, and be thou a guard unto them.

Preparation means you have done your homework regarding the requisite resources that are needed to embark on a venture, you have taken into consideration both internal and external circumstances that can derail your plans, when such preparation is inadequate, then defeat is imminent.

Luke 14:28-32 (KJV) For which of you, intending to build a tower, sitteth not down first, and counteth the cost, whether he have *sufficient* to finish *it*? Lest haply, after he hath laid the foundation, and is not able to finish *it*, all that behold *it* begin to mock him, Saying, This man began to build, and was not able to finish. Or what king, going to make war against another king, sitteth not down first, and consulteth whether he be able with ten thousand to meet him that cometh against him with twenty thousand? Or else, while the other is yet a great way off, he sendeth an ambassage, and desireth conditions of peace.

In the building industry, before a project is executed, adequate preparation is made regarding both technical and commercial feasibility of the project, drawings are prepared to determine the size, nature, height etc of the proposed project. Even cost estimate is prepared so that the sponsors of the project can make adequate plans for funding and to know the viability of the project. When this is not properly carried out such projects fail.

Also, in warfare, warring nations take inventory of their armoury, they take stock of their fighting men, they do intelligence and espionage works against enemy nations. All this is done to make sure they are fully prepared to engage in wars. In bible time, they still prepared horses for battle even though they knew that safety could only come from God:

> **Proverbs 21:31 (KJV)** The horse *is* prepared against the day of battle: but safety *is* of the LORD.

3. WRONG STRATEGY

Strategy is important in warfare. Wars have been lost and won based on strategy. For instance, I understand that Germany lost the 2nd world war because they flopped in their strategy by declaring war on the United State of America. That wrong strategy led to their defeat.

When Absalom declared war on his father in his attempt to overthrow David and become the king of Israel, he invited one of his father's closest advisers, Ahithophel, to help fashion out a strategy that will lead to David's capture:

> **2 Samuel 17:1-4 (KJV)** Moreover Ahithophel said unto Absalom, Let me now choose out twelve thousand men, and I will arise and pursue after David this night: And I will come upon him while he *is* weary and weak handed, and will make him afraid: and all the people that *are* with him shall flee; and I will smite the king only: And I will bring back all the people unto thee: the man whom thou seekest *is* as if all returned: *so* all the people shall be in peace. And the saying pleased Absalom well, and all the elders of Israel.

The scripture says that though Ahithophel strategy was better, however, because Absalom deployed another strategy as advised by Hushai gave David the opportunity to escape:

> **2 Samuel 17:5-13 (KJV)** Then said Absalom, Call now Hushai the Archite also, and let us hear likewise what he saith. And when Hushai was come to Absalom, Absalom spake unto him, saying, Ahithophel hath spoken after this manner: shall we do *after* his saying? if not; speak thou. And Hushai said unto Absalom, The counsel that Ahithophel hath given *is* not good at this time. For, said Hushai, thou knowest thy father and his men, that they *be* mighty men, and they *be* chafed in their minds, as a bear robbed of her whelps in the field: and thy father *is* a man of war, and will not lodge with the people. Behold, he is hid now in some pit, or in some *other* place: and it will come to pass, when some of them be overthrown at the first, that whosoever heareth it will say, There is a slaughter among the people that follow Absalom. And he also *that is* valiant, whose heart *is* as the heart of a lion, shall utterly melt: for all Israel knoweth that thy father *is* a mighty man, and *they* which *be* with him *are* valiant men. Therefore, I counsel that all Israel be generally gathered unto thee, from Dan even to Beer-sheba, as the sand that *is* by the sea for

> multitude; and that thou go to battle in thine own person. So shall we come upon him in some place where he shall be found, and we will light upon him as the dew falleth on the ground: and of him and of all the men that *are* with him there shall not be left so much as one. Moreover, if he be gotten into a city, then shall all Israel bring ropes to that city, and we will draw it into the river, until there be not one small stone found there.

Absalom made the biggest mistake of his life by listening and executing a faulty strategy, which later led to Absalom's defeat.

Absalom felt that Hushai's strategy was better than Ahithophel's and he executed Hushai's strategy. That strategy failed as it allowed David to escape to a neighbouring town.

2 Samuel 17:14 (KJV) And Absalom and all the men of Israel said, The counsel of Hushai the Archite *is* better than the counsel of Ahithophel. For the LORD had appointed to defeat the good counsel of Ahithophel, to the intent that the LORD might bring evil upon Absalom.

4. NOT ASKING FOR DIVINE ASSISTANCE

No matter your preparation, planning, strategy etc, it is important that you take your dreams to the Lord in prayers. When you look at this life, many who are competent, gifted, even anointed may not find it difficult to get to the top. Success in life is not entirely dependent on you, God still plays a very important role in the affairs of men:

> **Proverbs 21:31 (KJV)** The horse *is* prepared against the day of battle: but safety *is* of the LORD.

When you refuse to ask for help from the Lord, then God leaves you on your own:

Isaiah 22:9-11 (KJV) Ye have seen also the breaches of the city of David, that they are many: and ye gathered together the waters of the lower pool. And ye have numbered the houses of Jerusalem, and the houses have ye broken down to fortify the wall. Ye made also a ditch between the two walls for the water of the old pool: but ye have not looked unto the maker thereof, neither had respect unto him that fashioned it long ago.

When you leave God out of your plans, then you are making invitation for a big defeat.

There was a war between Judah and Israel that is recorded in the bible (2Chronicles 13: 1-18) for our learning. King Abijah, king of Judah had 400, 000 soldiers and yet defeated Jeroboam king of Israel who had 800,000 soldiers. This tells us that wars are not won on weapons of wars alone. Look at the way the bible described what led to Abijah's victory:

2 Chronicles 13:17-18 (KJV) And Abijah and his people slew them with a great slaughter: so there fell down slain of Israel five hundred thousand chosen men. Thus, the children of Israel were brought under at that time, and the children of Judah prevailed, because they relied upon the LORD God of their fathers.

5. SIN

As I have been saying in previous paragraph, you cannot win any life battle, if God is against you. If you are not born again or you are living in sins, the scripture says that you cannot enjoy the favour and blessings of God:

Psalm 7:11 (KJV) God judgeth the righteous, and God is angry *with the wicked* every day.

If you look at the defeat of Israel against Ai that I narrated above.

Apart from Israel being overconfident, there was also sin in their lives. They disobeyed God in taking the accursed thing, that is, one of them took something God had commanded them not to take, the result of that sin of course was a fatal defeat:

> **Joshua 7:12 (KJV)** Therefore the children of Israel could not stand before their enemies, *but* turned *their* backs before their enemies, because they were accursed: neither will I be with you anymore, except ye destroy the accursed from among you.

Having given reasons for defeat, please note that though you might have been defeated and you feel completely down. God does not want you to stay defeated. Even in the case of Ai, the children of Israel did not stay defeated. They recovered from defeat, you also can recover from defeat.

Let us now examine what you need to do to recover from any type of defeat:

1. KNOW WHY THE DEFEAT OCCURRED

When Israel was defeated in the battle against Ai, the first thing that Joshua did was post-mortem examination of what caused the defeat:

> **Joshua 7:6-7 (KJV)** And Joshua rent his clothes, and fell to the earth upon his face before the ark of the LORD until the eventide, he and the elders of Israel, and put dust upon their heads. And Joshua said, Alas, O Lord GOD, wherefore hast thou at all brought this people over Jordan, to deliver us into the hand of the Amorites, to destroy us? would to God we had been content, and dwelt on the other side Jordan!

Joshua had to go to God to ask God why is it that Israel could not stand in battle against their enemies? What Joshua was asking was God, why are we defeated? God in his infinite mercies, made it known to Joshua why Israel was defeated:

> **Joshua 7:10-11 (KJV)** And the LORD said unto Joshua, Get thee up; wherefore liest thou thus upon thy face? Israel hath sinned, and they have also transgressed my covenant which I commanded them: for they have even taken of the accursed thing, and have also stolen, and dissembled also, and they have put *it* even among their own stuff.

Once Joshua knew the reason for the defeat, he was able to address the cause and then at next opportunity Israel was able to defeat Ai. To you that is reading this book, I prophecy concerning you, you will recover from all losses and defeat in Jesus name, amen.

2. AVOID FAKE SYMPATHISERS

When David was chased out of the palace by his son, Absalom; Shimei of the tribe of Benjamin began to rain curses on David. Please note that king Saul was also from the tribe of Benjamin, hence, Shimei and his cohorts were not happy with David that king Saul lost the throne to David. Therefore, when David was chased out of the palace by Absalom, Shimei was more than happy that David had found himself in trouble:

> **2 Samuel 16:5-8 (KJV)** And when king David came to Bahurim, behold, thence came out a man of the family of the house of Saul, whose name *was* Shimei, the son of Gera: he came forth, and cursed still as he came. And he cast stones at David, and at all the servants of king David: and all the people and all the mighty men *were* on his right hand and on his left. And thus said Shimei when he cursed, Come out, come out, thou bloody man, and thou man of Belial: The LORD hath returned upon thee all the blood of the house of Saul, in whose stead thou hast reigned;

> and the LORD hath delivered the kingdom into the hand of Absalom thy son: and, behold, thou *art taken* in thy mischief, because thou *art* a bloody man.

Child of God, please beware of false sympathisers, some are happy that you have been defeated, so you need to be careful about those who come to you at your trying times. In this particular case, the table turned, and king David regained the throne. You would not believe that among the people that came to welcome king David was the same Shimei that had earlier cursed him:

> **2 Samuel 19:16-17 (KJV)** And Shimei the son of Gera, a Benjamite, which *was* of Bahurim, hasted and came down with the men of Judah to meet king David. And *there were* a thousand men of Benjamin with him, and Ziba the servant of the house of Saul, and his fifteen sons and his twenty servants with him; and they went over Jordan before the king.

David knew that Shimei was not a man to be trusted and therefore did not give him much space into his life.

3. ENCOURAGE YOURSELF

When Ziglag was ransacked and burnt down by the Amalekites, David, and the inhabitants of Ziglag lost family, houses, and business. David and the people of Ziglag wept and wailed until they could not find any more strength to weep. When everyone around David was disillusioned, not knowing what the future holds, David found strength in his God:

> **1 Samuel 30:6 (KJV)** And David was greatly distressed; for the people spake of stoning him, because the soul of all the people was grieved, every man for his sons and for his daughters: but David encouraged himself in the LORD his God.

It does not matter how terrible the defeat, if you are alive and well, you can recover from any loss. All you need is to approach the throne of grace and ask, what do I need to do to recover from this loss? And the almighty God will instruct you on what to do to recover from the loss. Joshua did and he recovered from the loss of Ai. David did it and he also recovered all that the Amalekites took from Ziglag. I believe God, if you approach God, he will also let you know what you need to do to recover from your defeat.

4. BE CAREFUL OF THE DECISIONS YOU MAKE AT THE TIME OF DEFEAT

When people go through defeat, their feelings and emotion run wild. There is a tendency not to make sound decisions that are based on sound reasoning and logic. This is because at this time, their reasoning abilities are beclouded with their emotions.

When David was chased out of the palace by Absalom. Ziba, servant of Saul, who David later instructed to take care of Mephibosheth in **2 Samuel 9** came around to show support to king David:

> **2 Samuel 16:1-2 (KJV)** And when David was a little past the top *of the hill*, behold, Ziba the servant of Mephibosheth met him, with a couple of asses saddled, and upon them two hundred *loaves* of bread, and an hundred bunches of raisins, and an hundred of summer fruits, and a bottle of wine. And the king said unto Ziba, What meanest thou by these? And Ziba said, The asses *be* for the king's household to ride on; and the bread and summer fruit for the young men to eat; and the wine, that such as be faint in the wilderness may drink.

However, David did not see Mephibosheth coming around to support him. David was curious to ask Ziba for Mephibosheth's whereabout, please hear Ziba's reply:

> **2 Samuel 16:3 (KJV)** And the king said, And where *is* thy master's son? And Ziba said unto the king, Behold, he abideth at Jerusalem: for he said, To day shall the house of Israel restore me the kingdom of my father.

With Ziba's reply, David took a decision regarding the property of Mephibosheth, this decision was based on reflex and emotions. He did not hear from Mephibosheth before taking a decision.

2 Samuel 16:4 (KJV) Then said the king to Ziba, Behold, thine *are* all that *pertained* unto Mephibosheth. And Ziba said, I humbly beseech thee *that* I may find grace in thy sight, my lord, O king.

King David had given all that Mephibosheth had to Ziba without hearing from him. However, David had to revert this decision on his return to Israel after hearing from Mephibosheth himself:

> **2 Samuel 19:24-27 (KJV)** And Mephibosheth the son of Saul came down to meet the king, and had neither dressed his feet, nor trimmed his beard, nor washed his clothes, from the day the king departed until the day he came *again* in peace. And it came to pass, when he was come to Jerusalem to meet the king, that the king said unto him, Wherefore wentest not thou with me, Mephibosheth? And he answered, My lord, O king, my servant deceived me: for thy servant said, I will saddle me an ass, that I may ride thereon, and go to the king; because thy servant *is* lame. And he hath slandered thy servant unto my lord the king; but my lord the king *is* as an angel of God: do therefore *what is* good in thine eyes.

2 Samuel 19:29 (KJV) And the king said unto him, Why speakest thou any more of thy matters? I have said, Thou and Ziba divide the land.

As you can see above, David had to cancel his earlier decision to give all that Mephibosheth had to Ziba. You also be careful of your decision during trying times so that you do not make very costly mistake that will be difficult to revert.

5. NEVER FORGET THOSE WHO STOOD BY YOU DURING DIFFICULT TIMES

David was a man that had his own share of difficulties. He suffered in the hands of king Saul. Two times his own children revolted against him, I am speaking about Absalom and Adonijah. At another time Sheba, the troublemaker, according to scripture also revolted against king David:

> **2 Samuel 20:1 (ASV)** And there happened to be there **a base fellow** (NLT – troublemaker), whose name was Sheba, the son of Bichri, a Benjamite: and he blew the trumpet, and said, We have no portion in David, neither have we inheritance in the son of Jesse: every man to his tents, O Israel.

When you study the bible very well you will discover that David never forgot all those who stood by him at difficult times. In the case of Jonathan, though Jonathan was dead by the time David ascended the throne he never forgot the good that Jonathan did to him at his trying time.

2 Samuel 9:1 (ASV) And David said, Is there yet any that is left of the house of Saul, that I may show him kindness for Jonathan's sake?

All that Mephibosheth enjoyed during the reign of king David was all because of Jonathan. Mephibosheth, lame at both feet, abandoned in a very remote village called lo – debar became someone whom God elevated to eat at the king's table. David did all this for Mephibosheth because of Jonathan:

> **2 Samuel 9:3 (ASV)** And the king said, Is there not yet any of the house of Saul, that I may show the kindness of God unto him? And Ziba said unto the king, Jonathan hath yet a son, who is lame of his feet.

> **2 Samuel 9:7 (KJV)** And David said unto him, Fear not: for I will surely shew thee kindness for Jonathan thy father's sake, and will restore thee all the land of Saul thy father; and thou shalt eat bread at my table continually.

David did not just show kindness to Jonathan, there was another of David's friends, called Barzillai, he was about 80 years when Absalom started his revolt against David. Barzillai was there for David when he was going through his trial, he was a genuine friend:

> **2 Samuel 17:27-29 (KJV)** And it came to pass, when David was come to Mahanaim, that Shobi the son of Nahash of Rabbah of the children of Ammon, and Machir the son of Ammiel of Lo-debar, and Barzillai the Gileadite of Rogelim, Brought beds, and basons, and earthen vessels, and wheat, and barley, and flour, and parched *corn*, and beans, and lentiles, and parched *pulse*, And honey, and butter, and sheep, and cheese of kine, for David, and for the people that *were* with him, to eat: for they said, The people *is* hungry, and weary, and thirsty, in the wilderness.

When David returned to Israel, Barzillai was also there to welcome him:

> **2 Samuel 19:33-35 (KJV)** And the king said unto Barzillai, Come thou over with me, and I will feed thee with me in Jerusalem. And Barzillai said unto the king, How long have

> I to live, that I should go up with the king unto Jerusalem? I *am* this day fourscore years old: *and* can I discern between good and evil? can thy servant taste what I eat or what I drink? can I hear any more the voice of singing men and singing women? wherefore then should thy servant be yet a burden unto my lord the king?

Barzillai rejected David's offer to come to Jerusalem to live with him due to old age, he rather recommended his son, Kimham, to live with the king in Jerusalem, and David obliged him:

2 Samuel 19:38 (NLT) Good, the king agreed. Kimham will go with me, and I will help him in any way you would like. And I will do for you anything you want……

David sowed goodness and kindness to people and no wonder God established his kingdom many generations after him:

Hosea 8:7 (KJV) For they have sown the wind, and they shall reap the whirlwind: it hath no stalk: the bud shall yield no meal: if so be it yield, the strangers shall swallow it up.

You also remember the good that people do to you and not forget them when the table turns in your favour. It shall be well with you in Jesus name, amen.

Chapter TWELVE

RENEW YOUR MIND

Ephesians 4:23 (KJV) And be renewed in the spirit of your mind. To realize the amazing you, you need to renew your mind, not just when you become a believer, you need to do this on daily basis. The battle for progress is always resisted by the power of darkness. The devil does not want anyone to make progress. He will fight it vehemently, he will not stop at anything to bring doubt, discouragement, fear etc to keep you from getting to the level God has designed you to be and this starts with the mind. Therefore, you need to renew your mind on a daily basis. Paul said that I can do all things through Christ that strengthens me (Philippians 4:13). What Paul is saying is that nothing will keep me from achieving that which God has placed in my heart, no hindrance can stop me. When you look at those who could not make the promise, they were shut out by their own thinking. They doubted the power of God to take them to the promised land and since they could not see these possibilities in their minds; there was no way they could have been able to see it in reality.

This doubt that the children of Israel experienced did not start when the spies were sent to the promised land but rather it had been building up even while they were in Egypt. Anytime they were confronted with a hardship, they will begin to say and think negative things about themselves, let us look at few examples:

1. WHEN PHARAOH RESISTED

When Moses approached Pharaoh and demanded freedom for the children of Israel, Pharaoh resisted and said:

> **Exodus 5:17 (KJV)** But he said, Ye *are* idle, *ye are* idle: therefore, ye say, Let us go *and* do sacrifice to the LORD.

When Pharaoh refused to let the children of Israel leave Egypt, he asked that the portion of their work be increased, some of the officers of the children of Israel were already agitated and could not even hold to confront Pharaoh, rather they began to regret their actions for even contemplating of freedom in the first place:

> **Exodus 5:19-21 (KJV)** And the officers of the children of Israel did see *that* they *were* in evil *case*, after it was said, Ye shall not minish *ought* from your bricks of your daily task. And they met Moses and Aaron, who stood in the way, as they came forth from Pharaoh: And they said unto them, The LORD look upon you, and judge; because ye have made our savour to be abhorred in the eyes of Pharaoh, and in the eyes of his servants, to put a sword in their hand to slay us.

2. AT THE RED SEA

When the children of Israel got out of Egypt and they were approaching the Red Sea and they saw the Egyptian armies behind them, they began to wish they had remained in Egypt:

Exodus 14:12 (KJV) *Is* not this the word that we did tell thee in Egypt, saying, Let us alone, that we may serve the Egyptians?

For *it had been* better for us to serve the Egyptians, than that we should die in the wilderness.

Anyone who cannot trust God especially in times of crisis and challenges, may find it difficult to see the power of God at play in their lives; this is because they will throw in the towel quickly, instead of holding on and see the salvation of the Lord.

3. IN THE WILDERNESS

Even in the wilderness, despite that they had seen the raw power of God, many of them could still not believe God to take them to the promise land. Look at when they needed food in the wilderness, some of them complained and doubted the ability of God to provide food for them:

> **Psalm 78:19 (KJV)** Yea, they spake against God; they said, Can God furnish a table in the wilderness?

> **Psalm 78:20 (KJV)** ....Can he give bread also? Will he provide flesh for his people?

Many of them have become perpetual complainants, they could not trust God, hence, when it was time to believe God for something bigger, they found it very difficult to trust God to help them to overcome the giants that they saw at the promise land. When you cannot trust God for little things, it will be very difficult if not impossible to believe God for bigger testimonies:

> **Psalm 78:41 (KJV)** Yea, they turned back and tempted God, and limited the Holy One of Israel.

Anyone who limits God cannot see the awesome power of God at work. Therefore, stop doubting God and God will come true for you in Jesus name, amen.

You will need to suspend your own thinking and trust the almighty God, who has the power to do all things for you to see the demonstration of power of God in your life:

Isaiah 55:7 (KJV) Let the wicked forsake his way, and the unrighteous man his thoughts……

Isaiah 55:8-9 (KJV) For my thoughts *are* not your thoughts, neither *are* your ways my ways, saith the LORD. For *as* the heavens are higher than the earth, so are my ways higher than your ways, and my thoughts than your thoughts.

God is able to do all things, so believe him.

Chapter THIRTEEN

CONNECT TO GOD'S GRACE

It is vain to sleep late and wake up early and still eat the bread of affliction **(Psalms 127:2).** Not everyone that works so hard have tangible result to show for it. One of the reasons why some work so hard and yet lack results is because such people lack the grace of God to succeed.

Without grace, labour will result in wasted efforts, may that not be your portion in Jesus name, amen. To lack grace, is to be without God's help, favour, or assistance. That means you are just labouring under your own efforts. That is a dangerous place to be, may that not be your portion in Jesus name, amen.

Look at Peter in **Luke 5:1-7**, he worked so hard, in fact, the scripture says that Peter and his colleagues toiled all night, yet they caught nothing. Not that Peter did not put in enough efforts and skills, but at that point he lacked God's grace and therefore he only laboured but his labour produced nothing. Grace when it is added to labour, produces outstanding results.

When Peter connected with grace, he got outstanding results that he had to beckon to colleagues in other ships to come and help because he alone could not draw the fishes, he caught to shore by himself.

When Israel as a nation lacked grace, they wandered in the wilderness for forty years. Please hear for yourself, what Moses said:

> **Deuteronomy 2:1 (KJV)** Then we turned and took our journey into the wilderness by the way of the Red sea, as the LORD spake unto me: and we compassed mount Seir many days.

This happened because God himself said to them do not go up because I am not among you:

> **Deuteronomy 1:42 (KJV)** And the LORD said unto me, Say unto them, Go not up, neither fight; for I *am* not among you; lest ye be smitten before your enemies.

When God is not with you, a short journey is unnecessarily prolonged like it happened for the children of Israel. A forty-day journey took extraordinarily long 40 years because God himself became the enemy of Israel.

Numbers 14:34 (KJV) After the number of the days in which ye searched the land, *even* forty days, each day for a year, shall ye bear your iniquities, *even* forty years, and ye shall know my breach of promise.

If you look up the latter part of the above verse in NLT it reads, you will discover what is like to have me for an enemy. What that means is that there is little you can achieve, when God is the one fighting against you.

The children of Israel found themselves wandering in the wilderness not because God could not take them to their destination at the right time but they themselves were the one who made God to fight against them through their unbelief and disobedience.

I would like to talk briefly about what grace does for the believer before analysing how-to walk-in grace:

WHAT DOES GRACE DO?

1. Grace makes sure that you find what you are looking for expeditiously:

Grace is important in achieving your goals. When the hands of God come upon you, what took some else more than 10 years to accomplish, when grace is involved it might take less than 5 years. Let us look at Joseph when he was invited to interpret Pharaoh's dream. God granted him unusual favour before Pharaoh. He was promoted to an enviable position, second to Pharaoh, in Egypt.

Genesis 41:40 (KJV) Thou shalt be over my house, and according unto thy word shall all my people be ruled: only in the throne will I be greater than thou.

Joseph's life changed same day, he was promoted, he was given Pharaoh's signet and he was clothed in fine linen and a gold chain was put around his neck. Pharaoh did not stop there. He also became the Pharaoh's in - law same day just because of interpreting a dream.

Genesis 41:45 (KJV) And Pharaoh called Joseph's name Zaphnath-paaneah; and he gave him to wife Asenath the daughter of Poti-pherah priest of On. And Joseph went out over *all* the land of Egypt.

What else are you going to call this accelerated promotion if not the grace of God. Grace makes you to find what others struggle to find with little or no efforts.

Grace is important in life's race, therefore connect to His grace and you see breakthrough beckoning to you with just the right efforts.

2. Grace makes sure that you receive guidance easily:

Guidance is important in achieving life goals, that is the reason young ones look for people to mentor them in life, so that they can receive the right and appropriate guidance. It might be good to have the right mentor, but more importantly, it will be great to receive God's guidance.

When David's family and others were taken captives by the Amalekites, David was not running to receive guidance from man, but he went to God first for direction.

1 Samuel 30:8 (KJV) And David inquired at the LORD, saying, Shall I pursue after this troop? Shall I overtake them? And he answered him, Pursue: for thou shalt surely overtake *them*, and without fail recover *all*.

Once David received divine direction to pursue those who raided his family, everything that followed was orchestrated by God. Though he received God's guidance. He also received man's guidance.

1 Samuel 30:15 (KJV) And David said to him, Canst thou bring me down to this company? And he said, Swear unto me by God, that thou wilt neither kill me, nor deliver me into the hands of my master, and I will bring thee down to this company.

David was greatly helped due to assistance he received from this slave, who was an Egyptian and was also part of those that raided Zig lag where David lived at the time.

The divine guidance that David received was key to David's success in recovering all that these band of raiders took away from him.

1 Samuel 30:16-18 (KJV) And when he had brought him down, behold, *they were* spread abroad upon all the earth, eating and drinking, and dancing, because of all the great spoil that they had taken out of the land of the Philistines, and out of the land of Judah. And David smote them from the twilight even unto the evening of the next day: and there escaped not a man of them, save four hundred young men, which rode upon camels, and fled. And David recovered all that the Amalekites had carried away: and David rescued his two wives.

Everything appeared easy for David in recovering all the enemy took from him because God was involved, so please before you take a major decision, ask God and he would guide you appropriately.

3. Grace helps you to bring down mountain with ease:

David did not struggle to bring down Goliath because grace was working for him. Many people are stopped by obstacles and difficulties in life. However, when grace is at work, obstacles becomes steppingstone to testimonies.

The scripture says that David prevailed over the Philistine with a sling and with a stone, and smote the Philistines, and slew him, but there was no sword in the hand of David (1Samuel 17:50).

You need the grace of God in your life, with the grace of God, you will see mountain crumble before you with minimal efforts. God said to Zerubbabel:

Zechariah 4:7 (KJV) Who *art* thou, O great mountain? before Zerubbabel *thou shalt become* a plain: and he shall bring forth the headstone *thereof with* shoutings, *crying*, Grace, grace unto it.

Grace is needed to see mountains crumble before you, so connect with grace!

4. Your Enemies are terrified because of you because of God's Grace upon your life:

One of the things that the nation of Israel enjoyed in their battles with enemy nations was God's grace:

> **Deuteronomy 2:25 (KJV)** This day will I begin to put the dread of thee and the fear of thee upon the nations *that are* under the whole heaven, who shall hear report of thee, and shall tremble, and be in anguish because of thee.

When Moses sent spies to Jericho to explore the land, the people of Jericho were so terrified that they lost every power to resist the incursion of their land by Israel:

> **Joshua 2:9 (KJV)** And she said unto the men, I know that the LORD hath given you the land, and that your terror is fallen upon us, and that all the inhabitants of the land faint because of you.

That is grace at work, that your enemies are afraid of you just because they heard of what your God had done for you in the past.

Joshua 2:10-11 (KJV) For we have heard how the LORD dried up the water of the Red sea for you, when ye came out of Egypt; and what ye did unto the two kings of the Amorites, that *were* on the other side Jordan, Sihon and Og, whom ye utterly destroyed. And as soon as we had heard *these things*, our hearts did melt, neither did there remain any more courage in any man, because of you: for the LORD your God, he *is* God in heaven above, and in earth beneath.

The nation of Jericho was thrown into panic because of the children of Israel.

If you want God to fight your battles for you, please connect to this grace!

5. Your desires are granted with ease when God's Grace is upon your life:

Nehemiah heard that the wall of Jerusalem had been broken down. He was concerned about his heritage. At this point, he was just a servant in the king's palace. When he appeared before the king to serve him drink, the king noticed that his countenance looked sad that day:

> **Nehemiah 2:2 (KJV)** Wherefore the king said unto me, Why *is* thy countenance sad, seeing thou *art* not sick? this *is* nothing *else* but sorrow of heart. Then I was very sore afraid.

Nehemiah told the king about the reason he wore a sad countenance and asked for the king to grant some leave to attend to the wall that was broken down in Jerusalem. One would think that this is a tough thing for a servant to ask from his master especially because Nehemiah was a captive in Susa. The king not only approved the leave that Nehemiah requested but also provided animal he was to drive to Jerusalem, the materials he needed for the works and letters to neighbouring governors to allow Nehemiah to have an easy passage as he embarked on his journey to Jerusalem.

Nehemiah acknowledged that this could not have happened if not the gracious hands of God that was upon him:

> **Nehemiah 2:8 (KJV)** And a letter unto Asaph the keeper of the king's forest, that he may give me timber to make beams for the gates of the palace which *appertained* to the house, and for the wall of the city, and for the house that I shall enter into. And the king granted me, according to the good hand of my God upon me.

Nehemiah's desires were granted due to the gracious hands of God that was upon him.

TO HAVE YOUR DESIRES GRANTED, CONNECT TO GOD'S GRACE NOW

How do you connect to God's Grace?

1. Accept Jesus Christ as Your Lord and Saviour:

When you accept the Lord Jesus Christ as your Lord and Saviour, you are accepting the finished work of Christ into your life, that means you receive the gift of salvation by the grace of God:

Ephesians 2:8 (KJV) For by grace are ye saved through faith; and that not of yourselves: *it is* the gift of God:

2. Avoid Sin:

Sin is what can rob you of the grace of God, therefore run away from sin. In Genesis chapter 39, Joseph fled from sin, because he knew that it could rob him of his destiny:

Romans 6:1 (KJV) What shall we say then? Shall we continue in sin, that grace may abound?

Numbers 32:13 (KJV) And the LORD'S anger was kindled against Israel, and he made them wander in the wilderness forty years, until all the generation, that had done evil in the sight of the LORD, was consumed.

Many could not enter the promise land because sin was found in them

3. Seek His Will for Your Life:

To have a breakthrough, you need divine guidance as I have previously enunciated. The scripture says:

Proverbs 3:6 (KJV) In all thy ways acknowledge him, and he shall direct thy paths.

When God is involved in your affairs, the extent of your breakthrough is unimaginable, therefore connect with his grace by letting him direct your plans.

4. Treat People Well:

When we talk about breakthroughs, God would have to use people to get you to his plans for you. He will not come down himself to help you. Many have missed their opportunities due to the ways that they treat their helpers. Men are the angels that God uses to achieve his plans. Be careful how you treat people.

Hebrews 13:2 (KJV) Be not forgetful to entertain strangers: for thereby some have entertained angels unawares.

If David had treated that Egyptian slave in 1Samuel 30 harshly he might have spent more time to locate those raiders. Please treat people well and God will help you in Jesus name, amen

5. Trust Him and Have Faith in Him:

To progress in life, you will need to exercise faith in God. The bible says:

Hebrews 11:6 (KJV) But without faith *it is* impossible to please *him*: for he that cometh to God must believe that he is, and *that* he is a rewarder of them that diligently seek him.

You will not be able to connect to God's grace without having demonstrating faith in him. The question is, what is faith?

Hebrews 11:1 (KJV) Now faith is the substance of things hoped for, the evidence of things not seen.

However, in layman terms, it is very simple, from the acronym F.A.I.T.H means: Forsaking all I trust him.

F – Forsaking

A – All

I – I

T – Trust

H – Him

From the above meaning, you have to suspend all other ways and completely trust the Lord and you will experience unimaginable testimonies in Jesus name, Amen.

May the good Lord help you to achieve your dreams in Jesus name, amen.

Chapter FOURTEEN

AMAZING GRACE FOR EXTRAORDINARY ACHIEVEMENTS

Everyone in life desires extraordinary results, everyone wants to succeed. No one wants to be a failure. However, not everyone succeeds in life. I have seen in this life, people with great potentials fail. I have also seen people with limited abilities succeeding. I used to have a friend, he had every opportunity to succeed, he was well connected some years ago with the mighty and powerful in the political space in Nigeria. Despite having such a great opportunity, he could not avail of this opportunity at the time for his benefit. I have also seen, some that no one reckons with, but because they were in the right place at the right time, you see doors opening for them. They seizing the moment and using such a great door to their advantage, the result is mind blowing, you can say that the latter achieved extraordinary results because of the amazing grace of God at work in their lives.

When grace is at work, you achieve beyond your own natural abilities, because it is the Lord himself that is propelling you forward. When you see an aircraft in the air moving with extraordinary speed, it is not the pilot that is making it to move with such a great speed, but the engine and capability of that engine that is doing the work, the pilot only regulate the speed. So also, it is with grace. Grace gives you exceptional capacity to move forward beyond your own natural abilities, look at the story of Elijah outrunning Ahab on a horse:

> **1 Kings 18:45-46 (KJV)** And it came to pass in the meanwhile, that the heaven was black with clouds and wind, and there was a great rain. And Ahab rode, and went to Jezreel. And the hand of the LORD was on Elijah; and he girded up his loins and ran before Ahab to the entrance of Jezreel.

That naturally is not possible, but the scriptures explained why that was the case, the hand of the Lord was on Elijah. Anything is possible when God is involved. It is important that God is involved in your life. While your gift will make room for you, the grace of God will take you beyond your capacity.

The scriptures gave account of one of Jonathan sons, who was lame as a result of an accident that he had when he was very young. He was living in a surburb of Israel called Lo-debar, no one reckoned with him. He was poor and abandoned at a remote village with little or no prospects at all. However, the grace of God located him. David woke up one day, nothing else occupied his mind but to do good to anyone still left in the household of Saul. Then he asked:

> **2 Samuel 9:1 (KJV)** And David said, Is there yet any that is left of the house of Saul, that I may shew him kindness for Jonathan's sake?

Then the people around the king said the only one that could know was Ziba, one of the servants of Saul. David summoned him quickly:

> **2 Samuel 9:3 (KJV)** And the king said, *Is* there not yet any of the house of Saul, that I may shew the kindness of God unto him? And Ziba said unto the king, Jonathan hath yet a son, *which is* lame on *his* feet.

As far as Ziba was concerned the king should not bother about such a one, as he had become invalid and could not be of any use to the king. David said I do not care whether he is lame or not, I want to show him the kindness of God. That kindness of God is what is called grace. Grace is a gift, you do not deserve it, it is not because of anything you have done, it is just the gift or kindness of God:

> **Ephesians 2:8 (KJV)** For by grace are ye saved through faith; and that not of yourselves: *it is* the gift of God:

Mephibosheth did not have any major input other than he belonged to the family of Saul and a son of Jonathan. David's kindness was a gift to Mephibosheth because of Jonathan. Do you know that as a child of God, the blessings of God was not because of anything that you have done? It is a gift of God to you because of what Jesus Christ did for us on the cross. Therefore, grace is an unmerited favour. I pray that you will encounter this amazing grace of God in Jesus name, amen.

I would like to enumerate what grace can do in the life of a man especially a believer in Christ:

1. GRACE IS A LIFTER

Have you seen the way a motor jack works? it helps you to lift a car that ordinarily you would not be able to lift on your own. It helps you to lift it with little efforts. There was no way Mephibosheth could have made it to the king's palace on his own, but due to benevolence of kind David, he was invited to begin to eat at the king's table:

> **2 Samuel 9:7 (KJV)** And David said unto him, Fear not: for I will surely shew thee kindness for Jonathan thy father's sake, and will restore thee all the land of Saul thy father; and thou shalt eat bread at my table continually.

Even Mephibosheth when he looked at himself, wondered what he had done to have merited the king's kindness. He compared himself to a "dead dog":

> **2 Samuel 9:8 (KJV)** And he bowed himself, and said, What *is* thy servant, that thou shouldest look upon such a dead dog as I *am*?

Do you know that the story did not end there? King David restored to him all that belonged to his father and grandfather and asked Ziba, his fifteen sons and twenty servants to begin to work for him. What a kindness? Whoa, this is unbelievable! No one would have expected the story of Mephibosheth to turnaround just like that. I pray for you that this is going to be your testimony in Jesus name, amen.

2 Samuel 9:9-11 (KJV) Then the king called to Ziba, Saul's servant, and said unto him, I have given unto thy master's son all that pertained to Saul and to all his house. Thou therefore, and thy sons, and thy servants, shall till the land for him, and thou shalt bring in *the fruits*, that thy master's son may have food to eat: but Mephibosheth thy master's son shall eat bread always at my table. Now Ziba had fifteen sons and twenty servants. Then said Ziba unto the king, According to all that my lord the king hath commanded his servant, so shall thy servant do. As for Mephibosheth, *said the king*, he shall eat at my table, as one of the king's sons.

2. GRACE HELPS YOU TO REIGN IN LIFE

When you look at the life of Apostle Paul, he said I am not worthy to be called an Apostle because I persecute the church of God:

> **1 Corinthians 15:9 (KJV)** For I am the least of the apostles, that am not meet to be called an apostle, because I persecuted the church of God.

He recognised that his becoming a witness for Christ was not because he deserved it, he put the credit on the mercy that God showed him. So, another word for grace is mercy. In Luke 15, the prodigal son also received the mercy of the father, he did not merit his father's goodness to him because he had strayed away from his father's presence. Paul recognised that as well and he said:

> **1 Corinthians 15:10 (KJV)** But by the grace of God I am what I am: and his grace which *was bestowed* upon me was not in vain; but I laboured more abundantly than they all: yet not I, but the grace of God which was with me.

Therefore, if you are a believer in Christ, Christ has paid all the price for you to reign in life:

> **Romans 5:17 (KJV)** For if by one man's offence death reigned by one; much more they which receive abundance of grace and of the gift of righteousness shall reign in life by one, Jesus Christ.

You must believe that your reigning in life is part of the package of salvation and you will see it manifest in your life in Jesus name, amen.

God took David from shepherding flocks in the wilderness to the palace. He also took Joseph from the prison to the palace, what is it that he cannot do? Your present situation does not matter, you are about to be taking to another level that if anyone told you, you would not believe it. Just believe and you will see God work on your behalf.

3. GRACE PROTECTS YOU IN TIMES OF CRISIS

When you look at the account of Mephibosheth as recorded in **2 Samuel 9**, he enjoyed extraordinary kindness from David. This kindness did not stop at Mephibosheth eating at king's table.

David's kindness spared Mephibosheth from being executed when the Gibeonites demanded for seven (7) heads of Saul's sons as the only thing that can pacify them.

2 Samuel 21:7 (KJV) But the king spared Mephibosheth, the son of Jonathan the son of Saul, because of the LORD'S oath that *was* between them, between David and Jonathan the son of Saul.

That is grace at work, David could have released Mephibosheth for execution, but for what Jonathan had done to David, David felt obligated to spare Mephibosheth from harm.

King Saul reneged the covenant that Joshua made with the people of Gibeon to spare them from being killed in Joshua chapter 9. Even though this covenant had been fraudulently obtained, God still honoured the covenant. This covenant notwithstanding, Saul had attempted to wipe the Gibeonites out. When David enquired of the Lord about the cause of the famine that erupted in his days, God said it was a result of what Saul did to the Gibeonites:

> **Joshua 9:15 (KJV)** And Joshua made peace with them, and made a league with them, to let them live and the princes of the congregation sware unto them.
>
> **2 Samuel 21:1-2 (KJV)** Then there was a famine in the days of David three years, year after year; and David inquired of the LORD. And the LORD answered, *It is* for Saul, and for *his* bloody house, because he slew the Gibeonites. And the king called the Gibeonites, and said unto them; (now

the Gibeonites *were* not of the children of Israel, but of the remnant of the Amorites; and the children of Israel had sworn unto them: and Saul sought to slay them in his zeal to the children of Israel and Judah.

The Gibeonites refused to be pacified by nothing but seven heads of the sons of Saul:

2 Samuel 21:6 (KJV) Let seven men of his sons be delivered unto us, and we will hang them up unto the LORD in Gibeah of Saul, *whom* the LORD did choose. And the king said, I will give *them*.

As children of the most- high, God has promised us divine protection. In Psalms 91, he promised us divine protection and that he will be our refuge in storms:

Isaiah 4:6 (KJV) And there shall be a tabernacle for a shadow in the daytime from the heat, and for a place of refuge, and for a covert from storm and from rain.

Not only that you shall be protected in storms, but you might even see thousands falling around you, but he said you will only see with your eyes, it shall not come upon you:

Psalm 91:7-8 (KJV) A thousand shall fall at thy side, and ten thousand at thy right hand; *but* it shall not come nigh thee. Only with thine eyes shalt thou behold and see the reward of the wicked.

What makes the believer special is nothing but the grace of God:

God is a good God to us the believers in Christ, look at what David did to Mephibosheth just because of David, that is the same that God has promised us as children of God. He said in Isaiah 43, I will protect you, and if it requires that I choose between you and the unbeliever, I will prefer to choose you and protect you from every harm.

Isaiah 43:3-4 (KJV) For I *am* the LORD thy God, the Holy One of Israel, thy Saviour: I gave Egypt *for* thy ransom, Ethiopia and Seba for thee. Since thou wast precious in my sight, thou hast been honourable, and I have loved thee: therefore, will I give men for thee, and people for thy life.

If David could do that for Mephibosheth, how much more our God. He will watch over and make sure that you are protected.

God spared Israel and sacrificed the first born of Egypt because of his love for Israel:

> **Exodus 4:22 (KJV)** And thou shalt say unto Pharaoh, Thus saith the LORD, Israel *is* my son, *even* my firstborn:

Do you know that till date; God still jealously protect Israel from every attack of the enemy? When you look at the Middle East today, Israel is surrounded by enemy nations. If they had the chance, they would want to wipe out the nation of Israel from the map. They could not do that because, God is in the midst of Israel:

> **Joel 2:27 (KJV)** And ye shall know that I *am* in the midst of Israel, and *that* I *am* the LORD your God, and none else: and my people shall never be ashamed.

All the efforts of the enemy nations to bring Israel down failed, I know that by the grace of God all efforts the enemy is putting together against you will also fail in Jesus name, so rest in God, you are protected!

Chapter

FIFTEEN

WAIT FOR GOD'S TIME

In **John 7:8(NLT)** Jesus said to his brothers who were nudging him to attend a Jewish festival known as "Festival of Shelters" to show his miracles, my time has not yet come. His brothers wanted him to be famous and felt the festival of shelters would be a great opportunity for Jesus to demonstrate his abilities to perform miracles.

Jesus, however, recognised the importance of timing. Timing is key to your success and breakthroughs. There are people that God has lined up to assist you in life and you can only meet them at a particular season of your life, if you run too fast you may miss that particular timing God has set for you to meet them. Therefore, though you want things to happen quickly, you must learn to wait on God for him to unveil his plans for your life.

Everything in life has been programmed to manifest at a particular time. The day you were born was the day God has programmed that you will be born. Look at even the Son of God, Jesus Christ, many prophets had prophesied his birth many years before his birth. He did not show up on the surface of the earth until when the fullness of time for his birth had come:

> **Galatians 4:4 (KJV)** But when the fulness of the time was come, God sent forth his Son, made of a woman, made under the law.

What of Jesus' death? His death also occurred at the appointed time God had planned:

> **Romans 5:6 (KJV)** For when we were yet without strength, in due time Christ died for the ungodly.

Many people are always in hurry to have breakthrough. Unfortunately, believers are also caught up in the web of impatience. They are in hurry to be rich, they are in a hurry to have children, they are in a hurry to build a house or to succeed in life. If you are hard working and you are doing all that God expects from you in order to succeed, then you may have to wait for God's time. At times God hides our blessings from us until the time it will give glory to his holy name. John the Baptist was hidden in the deserts for many years until he had fully matured and then God manifested him to Israel:

> **Luke 1:80 (KJV)** And the child grew, and waxed strong in spirit, and was in the deserts till the day of his shewing unto Israel.

When women get pregnant, they do not see the child until after nine (9) months. Why is it that God hide the baby in the womb for nine (9) months? God does that for the simple reason for the child to be formed, matured, grow all the vital organs of the body before bringing the child out for all to see. If a mother says I cannot wait I want to see my child say after 2 months, what that mother would get is a monster; and she would be very unhappy with the creature she will get. Therefore, you should know that there is always a period of waiting. That is the period when God is cooking your testimony, at that point you just have to wait until God perfects all things concerning you.

Beloved, God will make all things beautiful for you at his own time (**Ecclesiastes 1:11**). Please do not listen to voices telling you that you have waited enough, look for short cut. Please note that voice is not the voice of God, that is coming from the pit of hell. That is coming from the Devil and therefore never listen to the voice of the enemy. You are a child of God and he will come for you at the right time. That testimony will come, and it will no longer delay in Jesus name amen, please wait for it.

God can be trusted when you wait for him you can never be ashamed. Remember his past acts, God has never failed those who put their confidence in him, and he is not going to fail you too. Jesus told the disciples to wait for the promise of the Holy Ghost, did he keep his promise? Yes, he did:

> **Luke 24:49 (KJV)** And, behold, I send the promise of my Father upon you: but tarry ye in the city of Jerusalem, until ye be endued with power from on high.

> **Acts 2:1-2 (KJV)** And when the day of Pentecost was fully come, they were all with one accord in one place. And suddenly there came a sound from heaven as of a rushing mighty wind, and it filled all the house where they were sitting.

As you can see above, God kept his word, Hallelujah! God will keep his word concerning you also in Jesus name, amen. What of God's promise of a child to Father Abraham?

> **Genesis 18:10 (KJV)** And he said, I will certainly return unto thee according to the time of life; and, lo, Sarah thy wife shall have a son. And Sarah heard *it* in the tent door, which *was* behind him.

At the time God was speaking to Abraham, his natural strength had abated, his wife also was very old and there was nothing in the natural to say that what God had promised could come to pass. In fact, Sarah, Abraham's wife, started to laugh; one would not blame her for daring to laugh because naturally speaking, everything around them showed that what God said could not be performed:

> **Genesis 18:13-14 (KJV)** And the LORD said unto Abraham, Wherefore did Sarah laugh, saying, Shall I of a surety bear a child, which am old? Is anything too hard for the LORD? At the time appointed I will return unto thee, according to the time of life, and Sarah shall have a son.

You also might think that time has passed and that your dream are dashed already, if God could reverse the ageing process for Abraham and Sarah that they had their promised child according to what God spoke concerning them, then you are the next in line in Jesus name, amen:

> **Genesis 21:1-2 (KJV)** And the LORD visited Sarah as he had said, and the LORD did unto Sarah as he had spoken. For Sarah conceived, and bare Abraham a son in his old age, at the set time of which God had spoken to him.

Do you know the Shunammite woman was like that as well she had given up on having a child, so when Elisha, the prophet told her she was going to have a son, she retorted, do not lie to me man of God:

> **2 Kings 4:16 (KJV)** And he said, About this season, according to the time of life, thou shalt embrace a son. And she said, Nay, my lord, *thou* man of God, do not lie unto thine handmaid.

As far as this woman was concerned, she had made several attempts to have a child and they all failed. Maybe she had paid many physicians many consultations without any success, maybe she consulted many traditional healers and yet no success. Therefore, she had given up on the issue of having a child. She had accepted her fate that she was not going to have a child. Even though that was what was on mind, God turned that around, God proved to her that nothing is too difficult for him, that he is never late and that if you wait on him, things that you thought were impossible can become a reality all of a sudden. I would like to inform you, that testimony is on the way, please wait for it for it shall surely come:

> **2 Kings 4:17 (KJV)** And the woman conceived and bare a son at that season that Elisha had said unto her, according to the time of life.

Please never give up, never manipulate things just to get your desire. David had been trusting God for him to become the king of Israel. Instead of this coming to pass, David experienced great difficulties in the hands of king Saul. He ran from pillar to post, he was hungry and destitute, but he never gave up hope. An opportunity presented itself for David to take a revenge against king Saul:

> **1 Samuel 24:4 (KJV)** And the men of David said unto him, Behold the day of which the LORD said unto thee, Behold, I will deliver thine enemy into thine hand, that thou mayest do to him as it shall seem good unto thee. Then David arose, and cut off the skirt of Saul's robe privily.

In fact, the men around David said to him, this is a great opportunity to become the king, this man has been after your life, now seize this moment, no one is with the king, he is at a weak point now, no one would be able to come to his aid. One shocking thing happened, David refused to manipulate things so that he can quickly get to the throne, he waited on God to fulfil his words:

1 Samuel 24:6-7 (KJV) And he said unto his men, The LORD forbid that I should do this thing unto my master, the LORD'S anointed, to stretch forth mine hand against him, seeing he *is* the anointed of the LORD. So David stayed his servants with these words, and suffered them not to rise against Saul. But Saul rose up out of the cave, and went on *his* way.

David realised that if he manipulated things and he got to the throne quickly, the blessing might not last. So, David waited on God and when the time came, the people themselves came to David at Hebron to make him king:

2 Samuel 5:1-3 (KJV) Then came all the tribes of Israel to David unto Hebron, and spake, saying, Behold, we *are* thy bone and thy flesh. Also in time past, when Saul was king over us, thou wast he that leddest out and broughtest in Israel: and the LORD said to thee, Thou shalt feed my people Israel, and thou shalt be a captain over Israel. So, all the elders of Israel came to the king to Hebron; and king David made a league with them in Hebron before the LORD: and they anointed David king over Israel.

One of the qualities of a genuine child of God is patience:

Isaiah 28:16 (KJV) Therefore thus saith the Lord GOD, Behold, I lay in Zion for a foundation a stone, a tried stone, a precious corner *stone*, a sure foundation: he that believeth shall not make haste.

Look at Joseph, even though it took about 13 years for God's promise concerning him to be fulfilled, he waited patiently. He never lost hope, he did not manipulate things just for his dreams to come to pass. When Potiphar's wife tempted him, he refused the "bait" from the pit of hell:

Genesis 39:8-9 (KJV) But he refused, and said unto his master's wife, Behold, my master wotteth not what *is* with me in the house, and he hath committed all that he hath to my hand; *There is* none greater in this house than I; neither hath he kept back anything from me but thee, because thou *art* his wife: how then can I do this great wickedness, and sin against God?

You also hold on, trust him to keep his word. Do not fret yourself. Do not think God has abandoned you. He will show up at the right time:

Hebrews 10:23 (KJV) Let us hold fast the profession of *our* faith without wavering; (for he *is* faithful that promised;)

Do not approach the throne of grace double minded, that if this prayer does not work, then I will go for this alternative. If you do that, then you may never receive the divine intervention that you desire:

James 1:6-7 (KJV) But let him ask in faith, nothing wavering. For he, that wavereth is like a wave of the sea driven with the wind and tossed. For let not that man think that he shall receive any thing of the Lord.

Keep on trusting, keep on believing and your blessing will show up in Jesus name, amen:

Hebrews 10:35-37 (KJV) Cast not away therefore your confidence, which hath great recompence of reward. For ye have need of patience, that, after ye have done the will of God, ye might receive the promise. For yet a little while, and he that shall come will come, and will not tarry.

Lastly, the scripture says blessed are those who wait for his help (**Isaiah 30:18B**) When you wait for him, he is able to do for you beyond your imaginations, therefore, beloved please hold on, wait for him and he will show up for you in Jesus name, amen:

> **Isaiah 40:31 (KJV)** But they that wait upon the LORD shall renew *their* strength; they shall mount up with wings as eagles; they shall run, and not be weary; *and* they shall walk, and not faint.

When you wait on God, he mounts you up with wings like an eagle to soar high and fly over obstacles designed by the enemy to stop you. I see you getting to the top! See you there!

www.ingramcontent.com/pod-product-compliance
Ingram Content Group UK Ltd.
Pitfield, Milton Keynes, MK11 3LW, UK
UKHW020141250726
13967UKWH00002B/786